TEACHER'S
Discovery

COPYME prints

with new COPYME binding

Ten Basic Units for Middle School Spanish

Written by
Peggy Batty

Managing Editor
Wendy Hedstrom

Illustrated by
Juli Phillips

Page Layout Artist
Mila Ryk

ISBN: 0-7560-0440-3
SKU: B1384

Acknowledgements

In grateful appreciation to:

Dr. Ann Thomas, Ruthann McGovern, Bryn Byker, Kathy Demarest, Jack Humphrey, Warren Lottridge, Ruth Juntunen, Karla Rivers, Julie Lipke, Carolina Pittser, Meghan Wysong, Oriana Cadman, and Dr. Stella Moreno. Thanks also to Karen Kearcher, Peter Walton, Tammy Bowles, David Armeni, Luis Torres, Sara Marsyla, and other students at Lower Columbia College, who guided me toward this project.

Scope, Purpose & Organization

PURPOSE

- To introduce and reinforce basic high-frequency vocabulary and grammatical structures in a communicative format that allows for conversational interaction in the middle school classroom.

- To provide fun and interesting activities that will keep students engaged while they practice their Spanish vocabulary and conversation skills.

SCOPE AND ORGANIZATION

The book is divided into 10 units, with each new unit reinforcing vocabulary and grammar from previous units. Each of the units contains worksheets, answer keys, ideas for related activities, and assessments such as quizzes and projects. All projects also include rubrics for easy grading.

LEVEL

Level I middle school Spanish students.

How To...

TIME

Exercises and activities range from five to sixty minutes each. The projects range from one to four class periods each.

ADDITIONAL MATERIALS

Photos, scissors, tape, overhead transparencies, and an overhead projector.

INSTRUCTIONS

Refer to the teacher page at the front of each unit for detailed instructions for the activities and exercises in that unit. Suggestions for additional activities are also detailed on that page.

Table of Contents

1

Spanish-Speaking Countries

- Map Activities

- Country Research Travel Poster Project

UNIT ONE: SPANISH-SPEAKING COUNTRIES

Map Activities, pages 1-7:
- Copy and hand out pages 1, 2, 4-7 to your students.
- Together with the whole class read and review the information on page 1.
- Students complete the activities in order by using the maps on pages 4-7 to locate the 21 Spanish-speaking countries of the world.

Country Research Poster/Travel Brochure Project, pages 8-10:
- Copy and hand out pages 8-10.
- Assign this project following the completion of the mapping activities and some general discussion of geography and Spanish-speaking countries. Students research a Spanish-speaking country of their choice. They then design and present a travel poster based on what someone would discover there, using their five senses. Students will need two to four days to do the necessary research. The project outline and the grading rubric are on pages 9-10.

Additional Activity:
- Play the song "*Los Países Hispanos*" by Barbara MacArthur (found on the *Sing, Dance, Laugh and Eat Tacos* CD's and tapes, available through Teacher's Discovery). Middle school students love its catchy tune, and singing the song provides great pronunciation practice.

Spanish-Speaking Countries

Name: _____

Date: _____

Class: _____

Spanish is the official language of Spain. It is also the official language of most Latin American countries and of Puerto Rico. Hispanics comprise 20 percent of the current United States population. Most Hispanics living in the United States are bilingual, speaking both Spanish and English. Florida and the southwestern United States have large Hispanic populations, as well as other major U. S. cities such as Chicago and New York. More than 400 million people worldwide speak Spanish. The following countries claim Spanish as their official language:

Nicaragua	**Argentina**
Costa Rica	**Guatemala**
Venezuela	**Puerto Rico**
Mexico	**Panama**
El Salvador	**Honduras**
Ecuador	**Spain**
Uruguay	**Paraguay**
Cuba	**Chile**
Peru	**The Dominican Republic**
Columbia	**Bolivia**
Equatorial Guinea	

These 21 Spanish-speaking countries of the world are found in North America, Central America, South America, Europe, Africa, and the Caribbean. In addition to these countries where Spanish is the **official** language, there are many other countries in the world where Spanish is spoken as a second language by much of the population. Spanish is widely spoken as a second language in the United States by both Hispanics and non-Hispanics.

Spanish-Speaking Countries

Look at page 1 to get the list of the 21 Spanish-speaking countries of the world. Then, use the maps on pages 4-7 to find out which continents these countries are in. Write the country names under the correct continent name below.

NORTH AMERICA:

_____

CENTRAL AMERICA:

_____

_____

_____

_____

_____

CARIBBEAN:

_____

_____

_____

AFRICA:

_____

SOUTH AMERICA:

_____

_____

_____

_____

_____

_____

_____

EUROPE:

_____

NORTH AMERICA:

Mexico

CENTRAL AMERICA:

Honduras

El Salvador

Nicaragua

Costa Rica

Guatemala

Panama

CARIBBEAN:

Cuba

Puerto Rico

The Dominican Republic

AFRICA:

Equatorial Guinea

SOUTH AMERICA:

Peru

Argentina

Venezuela

Ecuador

Uruguay

Paraguay

Chile

Colombia

Bolivia

EUROPE:

Spain

Spanish-Speaking Countries -- North and Central America

Locate and circle the countries of North and Central America where Spanish is the official language.

Name: _____

Date: _____

Class: _____

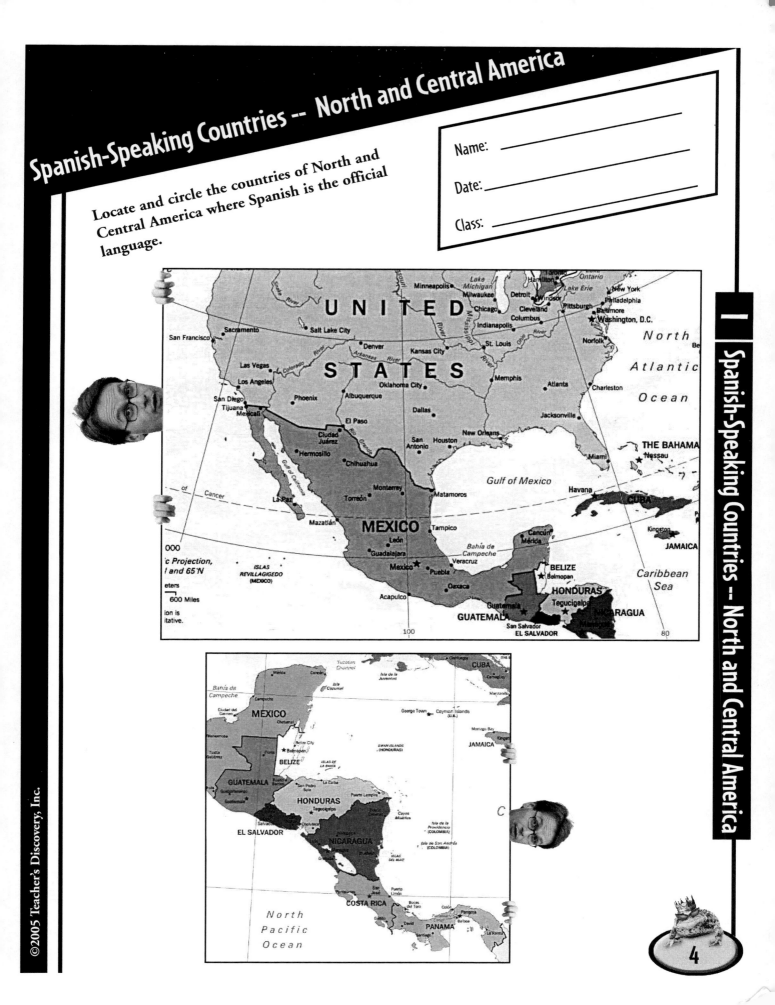

4

Spanish-Speaking Countries -- South America

Locate and circle the countries of South America where Spanish is the official language.

Name: _____

Date: _____

Class: _____

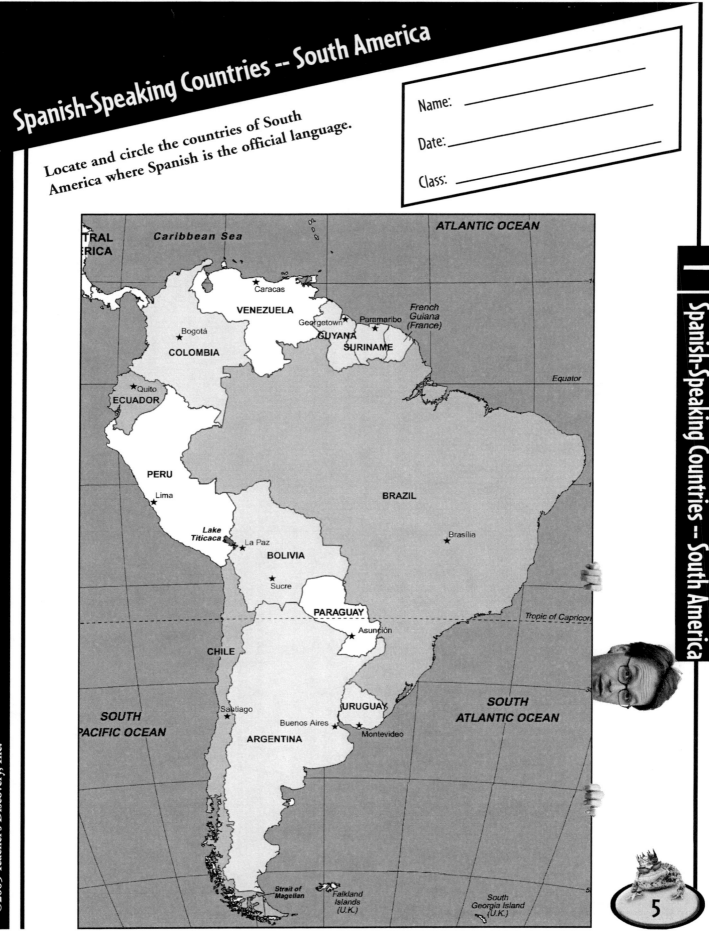

Spanish-Speaking Countries -- Europe

Locate and circle the countries of Europe where Spanish is the official language.

Name: _____

Date: _____

Class: _____

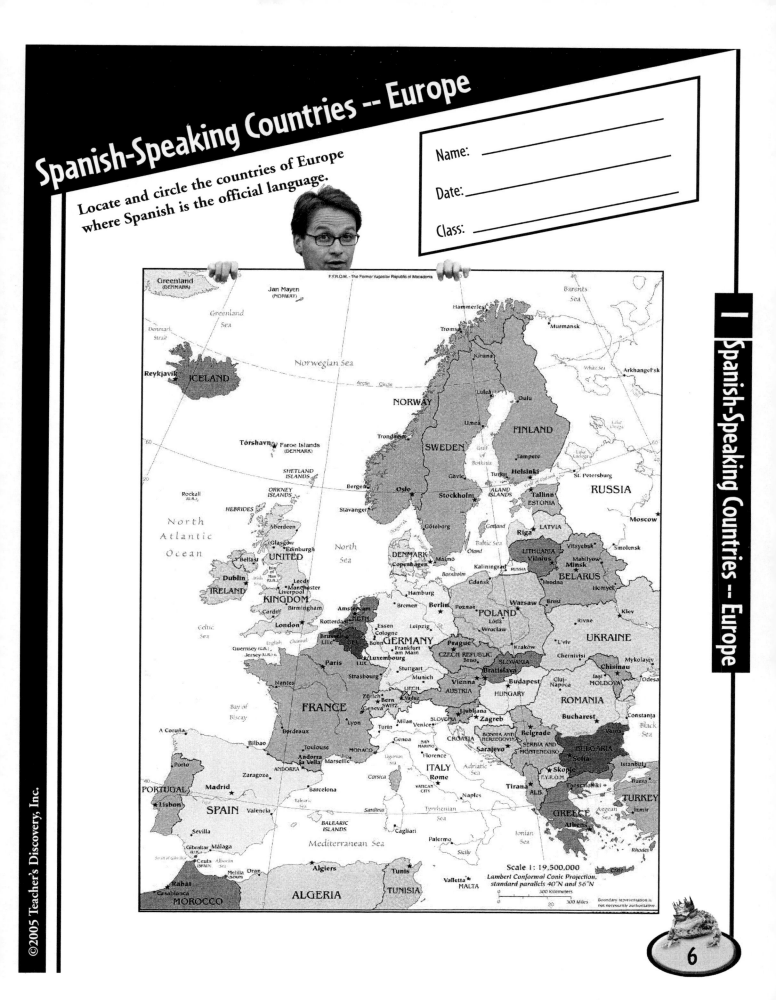

6

Spanish-Speaking Countries -- Africa

Locate and circle the countries of Africa where Spanish is the official language.

Name: _____

Date: _____

Class: _____

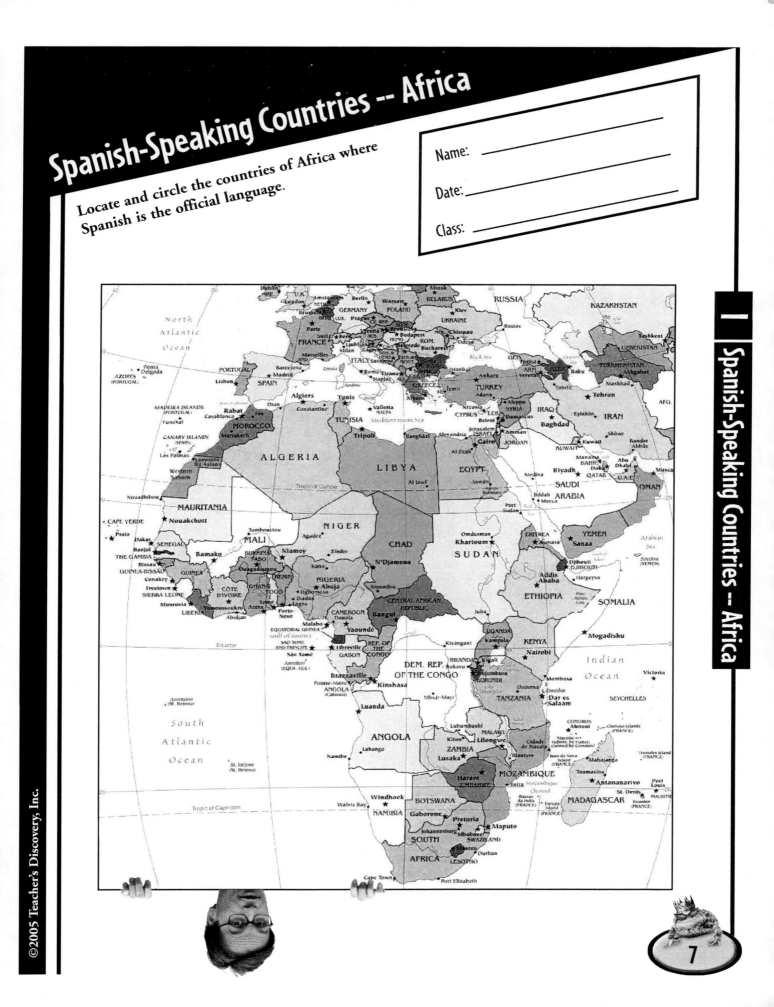

7

Spanish-Speaking Countries
Country Research Travel Poster

You are a travel company employee and you have been assigned a project to attract tourists to a Spanish-speaking country (pick a country from the list of the 21 Spanish-speaking countries on page 1). For this project, you will design a poster (no larger than 11"x14") and present it along with some information about the country you chose. Use the five senses (sight, hearing, touch, smell, and taste) as a guide to research your chosen country. Use a computer or go to the library for information.

The first part of your project will include an introduction to the country you chose and a written paragraph each about what can be seen, heard, touched, smelled, and tasted in that country. Write a paragraph each by answering the following questions in the order they appear. These paragraphs are worth five points each (25 points total).

A. **What can someone SEE in the country you chose?**
For example: Special attractions (museums, parks, pyramids), geography (lakes, sea, ocean, mountains, rain forest.)

B. **What can someone HEAR in the country you chose?**
For example: Native animals (where in the country are they found?), music (famous artists, musical instruments)

C. **What can someone TOUCH in the country you chose?**
For example: Geology (sand, rocks, water)

D. **What can someone SMELL in the country you chose?**
For example: popular foods, pollution, salty air, tobacco, fish, flowers

E. **What can someone TASTE in the country you chose?**
For example: fruits, vegetables, delicacies (animals, insects, plants, fish)

Spanish-Speaking Countries
Country Research Travel Poster Project

Name: _____

Date: _____

Class: _____

For this section, *choose five* of the following 10 topics to research on your country. Write down at least 4 sentences for every topic you choose. These topics are worth 5 points each (25 points total).

1. The capital of the country **and** the population of the country.
2. A famous person (living or dead) from the country and his/her profession.
3. The form of government the country has and its current leader.
4. **Two** of the country's major exports.
5. The country's major religion(s).
6. An important holiday in the country and the date it is celebrated.
7. The country's unit of currency and its exchange rate per U.S. dollar.
8. The name of a traditional song or dance from the country.
9. The general climate/weather of the country.
10. A major historical event involving that country.

The final section of your project must include:
- a map of the country   (10 points)
- a picture of the country's flag   (10 points)
- an acrostic poem using the country's letters (10 points)

The remaining 20 points will be awarded as follows:
- typing the report   (5 points)
- spelling and punctuation   (5 points)
- effort/time use in class   (10 points)

TOTAL   100 POINTS

Include a picture of something that can be seen in the country.

9

Spanish-Speaking Countries
Country Research Travel Poster Project
100 POINTS

Name: _____

Date: _____

Class: _____

A) FIVE SENSORY FACTS (FIVE POINTS EACH)

WHAT CAN YOU SEE? _____ /5
WHAT CAN YOU HEAR? _____ /5
WHAT CAN YOU TOUCH? _____ /5
WHAT CAN YOU SMELL? _____ /5
WHAT CAN YOU TASTE? _____ /5
               TOTAL SECTION A) _____ /25

B) OTHER FACTS (5 PTS EACH) MUST HAVE 5 OF THE FOLLOWING:

CAPITAL _____ /5
FAMOUS PERSON _____ /5
GOVERNMENT _____ /5
TWO EXPORTS _____ /5
RELIGION _____ /5
HOLIDAY _____ /5
CURRENCY _____ /5
SONG/DANCE_____ /5
CLIMATE/WEATHER _____ /5
HISTORICAL EVENT _____ /5
          TOTAL SECTION B) _____ /25

C) PROJECT DETAILS

MAP _____ /10
FLAG _____ /10
ACROSTIC POEM _____ /10
TYPED_____ /5
SPELLING/PUNCTUATION_____ /5
EFFORT/CLASS TIME USE _____ /10

_____

TOTAL ALL SECTIONS _____ /100

Greetings and Basic Vocabulary

- **Greetings Dialogue**

- **Basic Vocabulary**

- *Caminando y Preguntando* **Activity**

- **Greetings Quiz**

UNIT TWO: GREETINGS AND BASIC VOCABULARY

Greetings Dialogue and Basic Vocabulary, pages 13-14:
• Copy and hand out pages 13 and 14.
• Introduce the vocabulary words and the dialogue. Students read this dialogue out loud to practice basic greetings vocabulary.

Caminando y Preguntando Activity, page 15:
Pass out the ***Caminando y Preguntando*** sheet. The students move around the room asking two different people all three questions (this way, each student talks with two other students). The student who asks the question is to write the EXACT response in the box, then ask that student to verify the response by signing the sheet on the "*firma*" line.

Quiz, page 16:
Use the quiz to assess this unit.

Additional Activity:
After a couple days of practicing this basic vocabulary, students will be ready to write and perform basic dialogues and skits for the class. Encourage using props to make the dialogues and skits more interesting and to encourage creativity. Do not grade this initial activity as students will be more comfortable using their Spanish speaking skills. The performances also are a great listening comprehension activity for the rest of the class.

GREETINGS

Read the dialogue several times, then take turns playing the roles of María and Mario with a partner.

One of the first things we do when school starts is try to get to know our classmates. The following dialogue takes place between two Spanish-speaking students who are meeting each other for the first time.

Hola. Me llamo María. ¿Cómo te llamas?

Estoy bien, gracias. ¿Y tú?

¡Hasta luego, Mario!

Hola. Me llamo Mario. ¿Cómo estás, María?

Bien, gracias. ¿De dónde eres, María?

Adiós, María.

Soy de Puerto Rico. Y tú, Mario, ¿de dónde eres?

Soy de México. Mucho gusto, María.

San Juan

Puerto Rico

MEXICO

Greetings

Name: _____

Date: _____

Class: _____

¿Qué tal?	How are you?
excelente	excellent
muy bien	very well
mal	bad
muy mal	very bad
horrible/terrible	horrible/terrible
Hasta la vista.	See you later.
chao	goodbye
Hasta mañana.	See you tomorrow.
buenos días	good morning
buenas tardes	good afternoon
buenas noches	good evening/good night
por favor	please
de nada	you're welcome
perdón	excuse me
lo siento	I'm sorry

Greetings – Dialogue

Greetings
Caminando y preguntando

Ask two people in the class each of the three questions listed below. Record what they say, then have them sign their *nombre* on the line. When you are finished, return to your seat.

Name: _____

Date: _____

Class: _____

¿Cómo te llamas?	¿Cómo estás?	¿De dónde eres?
Firma: _____	Firma: _____	Firma: _____
Firma: _____	Firma: _____	Firma: _____

Greetings QUIZ

Name: _____

Date: _____

Class: _____

I. Vocabulario

Match the Spanish word or phrase with its English equivalent by putting the appropriate letter in the space provided (one point each):

1. *Buenos días* _____
2. *Por favor* _____
3. *¿Cómo te llamas?* _____
4. *¿Qué tal?* _____
5. *Perdón* _____
6. *Adiós* _____
7. *Hasta mañana* _____
8. *Lo siento* _____
9. *Hola* _____
10. *Soy de* _____

A. Hello
B. See you tomorrow
C. Goodbye
D. I'm sorry
E. Excuse me
F. I'm from
G. Please
H. Good morning/Good day
I. What's your name?
J. How are you?

II. Vocabulario/Reading Comprehension

Complete the following dialogue by providing the missing Spanish words. (two points each blank)
Hint: Always read the entire dialogue once before filling in the blanks!

Luisa: *Hola. ____ _____ Luisa. ¿Cómo te llamas?*

José: *Hola. Me llamo José. ¿ De _____ ____, Luisa?*

Luisa: *_____ de México. ¿Y _____?*

José: *Soy ____ Puerto Rico. _____ gusto, Luisa.*

Luisa: *Mucho _____, José. Hasta _____.*

I. Vocabulario

Match the Spanish word or phrase with its English equivalent by putting the appropriate letter in the space provided (one point each):

1. Buenos días — **H**
2. Por favor — **G**
3. ¿Cómo te llamas? — **I**
4. ¿Qué tal? — **J**
5. Perdón — **E**
6. Adiós — **C**
7. Hasta mañana — **B**
8. Lo siento — **D**
9. Hola — **A**
10. Soy de — **F**

A. Hello
B. See you tomorrow
C. Goodbye
D. I'm sorry
E. Excuse me
F. I'm from
G. Please
H. Good morning/Good day
I. What's your name?
J. How are you?

II. Vocabulario/Reading Comprehension

Complete the following dialogue by providing the missing Spanish words. (two points each blank)
Hint: Always read the entire dialogue once before filling in the blanks.

Luisa: *Hola.* **Me llamo Luisa.** *¿Cómo te llamas?*

José: *Hola. Me llamo José. ¿ De* **dónde eres,** *Luisa?*

Luisa: **Soy** *de México. ¿Y* **tú** *?*

José: *Soy* **de** *Puerto Rico.* **Mucho** *gusto, Luisa.*

Luisa: *Mucho* **gusto,** *José. Hasta* **luego/la vista/mañana.**

3

What Day Is It Today?

- **Months & Days of the Week Vocabulary**

- **Months & Days of the Week Activity**

- **Dates Activity**

- **Quizzes (Listening & Writing)**

UNIT THREE: WHAT DAY IS IT TODAY?

Days and Dates, pages 20-21:
• Copy and hand out page 20 to each student.
• Introduce the vocabulary for dates and days of the week with this page. A writing and speaking activity follows on page 21. Copy, hand out and have students complete.

Months of the Year and Important Hispanic Dates, pages 23-26:
• Copy and hand out page 23 and 24 to each student.
• Introduce the vocabulary for months of the year with page 23 before the students complete the writing and speaking activity on page 24. A list of important Hispanic dates is on page 25. Copy and hand out this list to students before they complete the writing activity on dates on page 26.

Quizzes (Listening and Writing), pages 28 and 31:
A listening quiz about birthdays is on page 28. Copy and hand out this page to your students. Then read out loud the script for this quiz on page 30. A writing and reading comprehension quiz for this whole unit is on page 31.

Additional Activites:
Use the overhead projector to show *realia* (schedules, menus, etc.) that are printed in Spanish and ask students to respond to questions about them.

Another activity is to ask a student a question in Spanish, such as *¿Cuándo es tu cumpleaños?*, as you toss him a small object like a bean bag. The student answers the question in Spanish, then tosses the bean bag to another student, asking him the same question. The activity continues until everyone has asked and answered the question. Use this activity to find out students' ages, favorite month, day of the week, etc.

What Day Is it Today?
¿Cuál es la fecha de hoy?

Below are the words you need to talk about days and dates in Spanish:

lunes	martes	miércoles	jueves	viernes	sábado	domingo
	1 PRIMERO	2 DOS	3 TRES	4 CUATRO	5 CINCO	6 SEIS
7 SIETE	8 OCHO	9 NUEVE	10 DIEZ	11 ONCE	12 DOCE	13 TRECE
14 CATORCE	15 QUINCE	16 DIECISÉIS	17 DIESCISIETE	18 DIESCIOCHO	19 DIECINUEVE	20 VEINTE
21 VEINTIUNO	22 VEINTIDÓS	23 VEINTITRÉS	24 VEINTICUATRO	25 VEINTICINCO	26 VEINTISÉIS	27 VEINTISIETE
28 VEINTIOCHO	29 VEINTINUEVE	30 TREINTA	31 TREINTA Y UNO			

Here are some additional words and phrases you need for discussing the week:

el fin de semana	the weekend
entre semana	Monday through Friday
de ( ) a ( )	from ( ) to ( ) {insert the day}
el lunes, el martes, etc	on Monday, on Tuesday, etc.
los lunes, los martes, etc.	on Mondays, on Tuesdays, etc.
¿Qué día es hoy?	What day is today?

What Day Is it Today?

Ayer, hoy, y mañana
(Yesterday, Today, and Tomorrow)

Name: _____

Date: _____

Class: _____

Practice saying and writing the Spanish days of the week with the following exercise.

Based on the day of the week given for either *ayer* (yesterday), *hoy* (today), or *mañana* (tomorrow), find the two missing days and write them in the blanks provided. Follow the model below:

Model: (**Hoy es viernes.**)   (**Mañana es sábado.**)   (**Ayer fue jueves.**)

1. *Hoy es jueves. Mañana es* _____.   *Ayer fue* _____.

2. *Hoy es martes. Mañana es* _____.   *Ayer fue* _____.

3. *Hoy es lunes. Mañana es* _____.   *Ayer fue* _____.

4. *Hoy es domingo. Mañana es* _____.   *Ayer fue* _____.

5. *Hoy es miércoles. Mañana es* _____.   *Ayer fue* _____.

6. *Hoy es sábado. Mañana es* _____.   *Ayer fue* _____.

7. *Hoy es viernes. Mañana es* _____.   *Ayer fue* _____.

Translate the following sentence:

Hoy es miércoles, ayer fue martes y mañana es jueves.

Practice pronouncing and writing the Spanish days of the week with the following activity.

Based on the day of the week given for either *ayer* (yesterday), *hoy* (today), or *mañana* (tomorrow), find the two missing days and write them in the blanks provided. Follow the model below:

Model: (**Hoy es viernes.**)   (**Mañana es sábado.**)   (**Ayer fue jueves.**)

1. *Hoy es jueves. Mañana es* __viernes__ .   *Ayer fue* __miércoles__ .

2. *Hoy es martes. Mañana es* __miércoles__ .   *Ayer fue* __lunes__ .

3. *Hoy es lunes. Mañana es* __martes__ .   *Ayer fue* __domingo__ .

4. *Hoy es domingo. Mañana es* __lunes__ .   *Ayer fue* __sábado__ .

5. *Hoy es miércoles. Mañana es* __jueves__ .   *Ayer fue* __martes__ .

6. *Hoy es sábado. Mañana es* __domingo__ .   *Ayer fue* __viernes__ .

7. *Hoy es viernes. Mañana es* __sábado__ .   *Ayer fue* __jueves__ .

Translate the following sentence:

Hoy es miércoles, ayer fue martes y mañana es jueves.

Today is Wednesday, yesterday was Tuesday and tomorrow is Thursday.

What Day Is it Today?
Los meses del año
(The Months of the Year)

Name: _____

Date: _____

Class: _____

Below are the Spanish words for the months of the year:

enero	(January)
febrero	(February)
marzo	(March)
abril	(April)
mayo	(May)
junio	(June)
julio	(July)
agosto	(August)
septiembre	(September)
octubre	(October)
noviembre	(November)
diciembre	(December)

In Spanish, the date is expressed using the following four-part formula:

el + (number) + de + (month)

For example: June 2 would be expressed as: *el dos de junio*
August 7 would be expressed as: *el siete de agosto*

There is one exception to this rule: When expressing the first day of a month, Spanish uses the word *"primero:" el primero de abril.* This is why on the calendar on the preceding page, number one is written as *"primero."*

For example:

¿Cuál es la fecha de hoy?   *Hoy es el primero de enero.*
What is the date today?   Today is January 1.

23

What Day Is it Today?
Los meses del año
(The Months of the Year)

Name: _____

Date: _____

Class: _____

You already know how to ask for several types of personal information from someone (*¿Cómo te llamas?, ¿Cómo estás?/¿Qué tal?, and ¿De dónde eres?*). Now you can also find out the date of someone's birthday by asking the question, *"¿Cuándo es tu cumpleaños?"*

María: *¿Cuándo es tu cumpleaños, Juan?*
(When is your birthday, Juan?)

Juan: *Mi cumpleaños es el seis de agosto.*
(My birthday is August 6.)

Ask seven of your classmates, in Spanish, when their birthdays are, and record the information below. Don't forget to use the four-part date formula (**el + (number) + de + (month)**) when recording your classmates' information and when responding to your classmates' questions.

1. *El cumpleaños de* _____ *es el* _____ *de* _____.

2. *El cumpleaños de* _____ *es* __ _____ __ _____.

3. *El cumpleaños de* _____ *es* __ _____ __ _____.

4. *El cumpleaños de* _____ *es* __ _____ __ _____.

5. *El cumpleaños de* _____ *es* __ _____ __ _____.

6. *El cumpleaños de* _____ *es* __ _____ __ _____.

7. *El cumpleaños de* _____ *es* __ _____ __ _____.

When you want to ask someone how old they are in Spanish, you ask, *"¿Cuántos años tienes?"* The answer is *"Tengo _____ años"*, (the person's age will go in the blank). Practice asking several classmates how old they are, and tell them how old you are.

24

What Day Is it Today?

Listed below are some important dates and holidays in Hispanic countries.

Name: _____

Date: _____

Class: _____

Month	Holiday	Country	Date
January	3 Kings Day	Mexico/Spain	January 6
February	Flag Day	Mexico	February 5
March	President's Day	Mexico	March 21
April	Easter	all	date will vary
May	Easter	all	date will vary
June	John the Baptist Day	all	June 24
July	Venezuelan Independence Day	Venezuela	July 5
August	Feast of the Assumption	all	August 15
September	Battle of Boquerón Independence Day	Paraguay Mexico	September 29 September 16
October	Día de la Raza	Mexico	October 12
November	Day of the Dead	Mexico	November 1 & 2
December	Christmas	all	December 25

What Day Is it Today?

Convert the dates of the holidays into Spanish. Don't forget to use the four-part date formula (el + (number) + de + (month))

Name: _____

Date: _____

Class: _____

1. Christmas Day _____

2. John the Baptist Day _____

3. Feast of the Assumption _____

4. Three Kings Day _____

5. *Cinco de mayo* _____

6. President's Day _____

7. Venezuelan Independence Day _____

8. Flag Day _____

9. *Día de la Raza* _____

10. Battle of Boquerón _____

11. *Día de los Muertos* (two dates) _____

12. Day of the Dead _____

©2005 Teacher's Discovery, Inc.

26

1. Christmas Day _____ *el veinticinco (veinte y cinco) de diciembre*

2. John the Baptist Day _____ *el veinticuatro (veinte y cuatro) de junio*

3. Feast of the Assumption _____ *el quince de agosto*

4. Three Kings Day _____ *el seis de enero*

5. *Cinco de mayo* _____ *el cinco de mayo*

6. President's Day _____ *el veintiuno (veinte y uno) de marzo*

7. Venezuelan Independence Day _____ *el cinco de julio*

8. Flag Day _____ *el cinco de febrero*

9. *Día de la Raza* _____ *el doce de octubre*

10. Battle of Boquerón _____ *el veintinueve de septiembre*

11. *Día de los Muertos* (two dates) _____ *el primero de noviembre*

12. Day of the Dead _____ *el dos de noviembre*

27

What Day Is It Today?
QUIZ – EL CALENDARIO

Name: _____

Date: _____

Class: _____

I. Listening (10 points)

Your teacher will read you some birthdates. Listen to the birthdates given, th
person with the birthdate. The names you will use are listed below.

Ana   **Jesús**   **Humberto**   **David**   **Rosa**

1. August 9 _____

2. June 1 _____

3. December 6_____

4. January 23_____

5. March 15_____

II. Matching (10 points)

Match the English vocabulary words with their Spanish equivalents:

1. the weekend _____   **a.** *ayer*

2. today _____   **b.** *la semana*

3. yesterday _____   **c.** *los sábados*

4. birthday _____   **d.** *hoy*

5. Monday-Friday _____   **e.** *el jueves*

6. on Thursday _____   **f.** *el mes*

7. tomorrow _____   **g.** *el fin de semana*

8. on Saturdays _____   **h.** *el cumpleaños*

9. week _____   **i.** *mañana*

10. month _____   **j.** *entre semana*

I. Listening (10 points)

Listen to the birthdates given on page 30, then match the person with the birthdate. The names you will use are listed below.

Ana **Jesús** **Humberto** **David** **Rosa**

1. August 9 _____ *Humberto*

2. June 1 _____ *Rosa*

3. December 6 _____ *Ana*

4. January 23 _____ *Jesús*

5. March 15 _____ *David*

II. Matching (10 points)

Match the English vocabulary words with their Spanish equivalents:

1. the weekend   __G__   a. *ayer*

2. today   __D__   b. *la semana*

3. yesterday   __A__   c. *los sábados*

4. birthday   __H__   d. *hoy*

5. Monday-Friday   __J__   e. *el jueves*

6. on Thursday   __E__   f. *el mes*

7. tomorrow   __I__   g. *el fin de semana*

8. on Saturdays   __C__   h. *el cumpleaños*

9. week   __B__   i. *mañana*

10. month   __F__   j. *entre semana*

1. Hola. Me llamo Ana. Mi cumpleaños es el seis de diciembre.

2. Buenos días. Soy Humberto. Mi cumpleaños es el nueve de agosto.

3. Me llamo David, y mi cumpleaños es el quince de marzo.

4. Soy Rosa. La fecha de mi cumpleaños es el primero de junio.

5. Me llamo Jesús, y mi cumpleaños es el veintitrés de enero.

What Day Is it Today?
Quiz - El calendario

Name: _____

Date: _____

Class: _____

III. Vocabulario (19 points) Spelling counts here!!!!

1. List, in order, the 12 months of the year in Spanish. Start with the word for January.

1._____   7._____

2._____   8._____

3._____   9._____

4._____   10._____

5._____   11._____

6._____   12._____

2. List, in order of the Spanish calendar, the seven days of the week.

1._____

2._____

3._____

4._____

5._____

6._____

7._____

IV. Reading Comprehension (Eight points)

Read the following paragraph, then answer the questions in English.

Hola. Me llamo Miguel. Mi número de teléfono es dos-dos-tres-nueve-cinco-dos-cuatro. Tengo catorce años. Mi cumpleaños es el primero de enero. Soy de la capital de El Salvador. Mucho gusto.

1. What number appears most frequently in Miguel's phone number?

_____

2. When is Miguel's birthday?

_____

3. How old is Miguel?

_____

4. Where is Miguel from?

_____

III. Vocabulario (19 points) Spelling counts here!!!!

1. List, in order, the 12 months of the year in Spanish. Start with the word for January.

1. enero
2. febrero
3. marzo
4. abril
5. mayo
6. junio
7. julio
8. agosto
9. septiembre
10. octubre
11. noviembre
12. diciembre

2. List, in order of the Spanish calendar, the seven days of the week.

1. lunes
2. martes
3. miércoles
4. jueves
5. viernes
6. sábado
7. domingo

IV. Reading Comprehension (Eight points)

Read the following paragraph, then answer the questions in English.

Hola. Me llamo Miguel. Mi número de teléfono es dos-dos-tres-nueve-cinco-dos-cuatro. Tengo catorce años. Mi cumpleaños es el primero de enero. Soy de la capital de El Salvador. Mucho gusto.

1. What number appears most frequently in Miguel's phone number?

two

2. When is Miguel's birthday?

January 1st.

3. How old is Miguel?

14

4. Where is Miguel from?

(the capital of) El Salvador

32

4

What Time Is It?

- **Telling-the-Time Vocabulary and Exercises**

- **Quiz (Listening & Writing)**

UNIT FOUR: WHAT TIME IS IT?

Telling-the-Time Vocabulary and Activities, pages 35-40:

Copy, hand out and review with your students the telling-the-time vocabulary on page 35. Three activities that increase in difficulty follow on pages 36 ("on the dot"), 38 ("quarter and half-past"), and 40 ("around the clock").

Quizzes (Listening and Writing), pages 42 and 45:

Copy and hand out the listening quiz about telling the time on page 42 before you read out loud the script for this quiz on page 44 to the class. A writing quiz follows on page 45.

Additional Activities:

Telling time bingo is a great activity to use with this unit. Look for it in educational toy stores such as Zany Brainy, or make your own. You simply need to call the times in Spanish.

Bingo games are also good for practicing numbers to 100.

Use *realia,* such as the school schedule, to have conversations about telling time. Copy the school's schedule onto an overhead transparency, then ask students questions such as *¿A qué hora empieza la primera hora?.*

Another good activity is to have students make watches out of construction paper, then tape them to their wrists. Students then circulate the room asking each other *¿Qué hora es?.*

What Time Is It?

You already know the numbers from 1-31, which you used to express the date in Spanish. Now here are the numbers from 32 to 59, which will enable you tell time in Spanish.

Treinta	Cuarenta	Cincuenta
treinta y uno	cuarenta y uno	cincuenta y uno
treinta y dos	cuarenta y dos	cincuenta y dos
treinta y tres	cuarenta y tres	cincuenta y tres
treinta y cuatro	cuarenta y cuatro	cincuenta y cuatro
treinta y cinco	cuarenta y cinco	cincuenta y cinco
treinta y seis	cuarenta y seis	cincuenta y seis
treinta y siete	cuarenta y siete	cincuenta y siete
treinta y ocho	cuarenta y ocho	cincuenta y ocho
treinta y nueve	cuarenta y nueve	cincuenta y nueve

As you see, once you have mastered the Spanish words for 30, 40 and 50, the rest is easy - just add *"y"* and a number from *uno* to *nueve!*

Telling time in Spanish

¿Qué hora es?
(What time is it?)

What Time Is It?
¿Qué hora es?

Look at the times on the clocks below and write the numbers out longhand in Spanish.

Name: _____

Date: _____

Class: _____

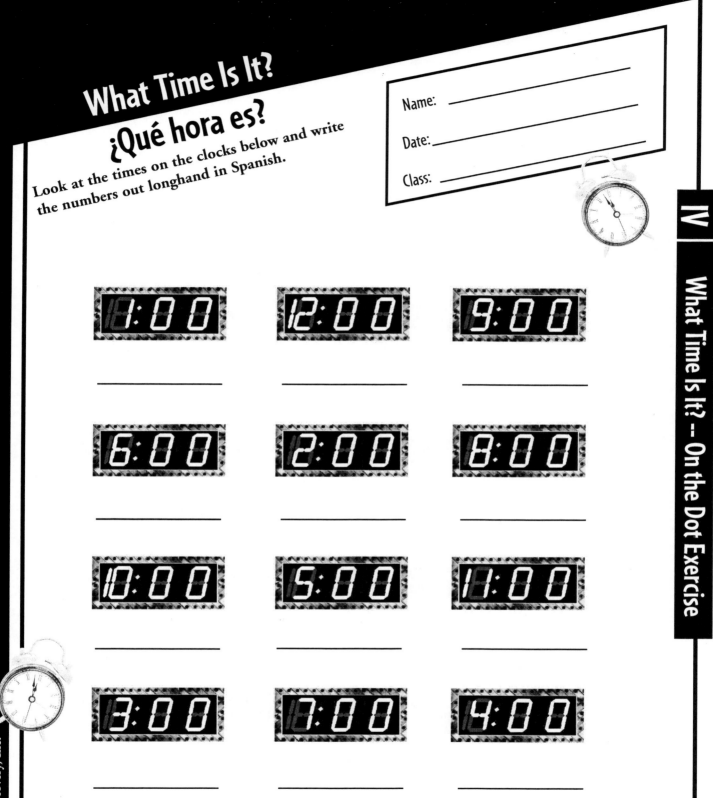

```
1:00          12:00          9:00
```
_____   _____   _____

```
6:00           2:00           8:00
```
_____   _____   _____

```
10:00          5:00           11:00
```
_____   _____   _____

```
3:00           7:00           4:00
```
_____   _____   _____

When the hour is "on the dot" we say *"en punto"* in Spanish. To practice with this phrase, go back and add the Spanish phrase for "on the dot" to each of the clocks you just worked on.

¿Qué hora es?

Look at the times on the clocks below and write the numbers out longhand in Spanish.

Es la una (en punto)

Son las doce (en punto)

Son las nueve (en punto)

Son las seis (en punto)

Son las dos (en punto)

Son las ocho (en punto)

Son las diez (en punto)

Son las cinco (en punto)

Son las once (en punto)

Son las tres (en punto)

Son las siete (en punto)

Son las cuatro (en punto)

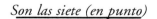
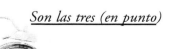

What Time Is It?
¿Qué hora es?

Name: _____

Date: _____

Class: _____

What do we do when the time is not *"en punto"*? In Spanish, as in English, the minutes are simply added to the hour. If it is 1:12, we would say, *"Es la una y doce."* If it is 2:12, we would say, *"Son las dos y doce."*

When the time is "quarter past" or "half past" the hour, use the following phrases:

"y cuarto" = **quarter after**   *"y media"* = **half past**

Use this new vocabulary to give the times of the clocks below.

_____

_____

_____

_____

_____

_____

_____

_____

_____

What do we do when the time is not *"en punto"*? In Spanish, as in English, the minutes are simply added to the hour. If it is 1:12, we would say, *"Es la una y doce."* If it is 2:12, we would say, *"Son las dos y doce."*

When the time is "quarter past" or "half past" the hour, use the following phrases:

"y cuarto" = **quarter after**   *"y media"* = **half past**

Use this new vocabulary to give the times of the clocks below.

Son las tres y diecisiete

Son las nueve y veintisiete

Son las siete y nueve

Es la una y veinticuatro

Son las cuatro y cuarto

Son las seis y media

Son las diez y cuarto

Son las once y veintidós

Son las dos y media

What Time Is It?
¿Qué hora es?

Name: _____

Date: _____

Class: _____

When the time is more than half past the hour (between 31 minutes and 59 minutes past the hour), there are two ways to express this in Spanish.

The simplest way is to simply add the minutes to the hour, as you did in the previous exercises.

For example:

"It's 1:55."
"Es la una y cincuenta y cinco."

"It's 12:45."
"Son las doce y cuarenta y cinco."

A different way to express this is to count up to the next hour, and then subtract the minutes left until that hour strikes.

For example:

"Es la una y cincuenta y cinco" could also be expressed as: *"Son las dos menos cinco."*

Use both the adding and subtracting method to give the time of the clocks below. Don't forget to spell your numbers in Spanish.

_____
_____
_____

_____
_____
_____

When the time is more than half past the hour (between 31 minutes and 59 minutes past the hour), there are two ways to express this in Spanish.

The simplest way is to simply add the minutes to the hour, as you did in the previous exercises.

For example:

"It's 1:55."
"Es la una y cincuenta y cinco."

"It's 12:45."
"Son las doce y cuarenta y cinco."

A different way to express this is to count up to the next hour, and then subtract the minutes left until that hour strikes.

For example:

"Es la una y cincuenta y cinco" could also be expressed as: *"Son las dos menos cinco."*

Use both the adding or subtracting method to give the time on the clocks below. Don't forget to spell your numbers in Spanish!

Son las diez menos cuarto/Son las nueve y cuarenta y cinco

Son las cinco menos veintitrés/Son las cuatro y treinta y siete siete

Son las dos menos ocho/ Es la una y cincuenta y dos

Son las doce menos uno/ Son las once y cincuenta y nueve

Son las tres menos catorce/Son las dos y cuarenta y seis

Son las siete menos veintidós/Son las seis y treinta y ocho

What Time Is It?
Quiz
¿Qué hora es?

Name: _____

Date: _____

Class: _____

PRIMERA PARTE: Write in digital form the times you hear your teacher say in Spanish (two points each):

1. `18:88`

2. `18:88`

3. `18:88`

4. `18:88`

5. `18:88`

6. `18:88`

7. `18:88`

8. `18:88`

9. `18:88`

QUIZ
¿Qué hora es?

PRIMERA PARTE: Write in digital form the times you hear your teacher say in Spanish (two points each):

1. 9:55
2. 1:00
3. 12:02
4. 7:14
5. 8:37
6. 8:45
7. 4:30
8. 1:30
9. 7:45

What Time Is It?

Quiz
Script for Listening Section

Name: _____

Date: _____

Class: _____

1. Son las diez menos cinco.

2. Es la una en punto.

3. Son las doce y dos.

4. Son las siete y catorce.

5. Son las ocho y treinta y siete.

6. Son las nueve menos cuarto.

7. Son las cuatro y media.

8. Es la una y media.

9. Son las ocho menos quince.

What Time Is It?
QUIZ
¿Qué hora es?

SEGUNDA PARTE: Read the following times of day in Spanish and indicate numerically (as it would look on a digital clock) what time it is (two points each):

1. Son las cuatro y cuarto.   _____

2. Es la una y veinte.   _____

3. Son las tres menos diez.   _____

4. Es la una menos cinco.   _____

5. Son las siete en punto.   _____

TERCERA PARTE: Write out in Spanish words the times indicated below (two points each):

1. `1:15`

_____

_____

2. `7:10`

_____

_____

3. `11:05`

_____

_____

4. `9:00`

_____

_____

5. `3:50`

_____

_____

6. `6:20`

_____

_____

QUIZ
¿Qué hora es?

SEGUNDA PARTE: Read the following times of day in Spanish and indicate numerically (as it would look on a digital clock) what time it is (two points each):

1. Son las cuatro y cuarto.   _____4:15_____

2. Es la una y veinte.   _____1:20_____

3. Son las tres menos diez.   _____2:50_____

4. Es la una menos cinco.   _____12:55_____

5. Son las siete en punto.   _____7:00_____

TRICERA PARTE: Write out in Spanish words the times indicated below (two points each):

1.

Es la una y cuarto
_(or)_
Es la una y quince

2.

Son las siete y diez

3.

Son las once y cinco

4.

Son las nueve
(en punto)

5.

Son las tres y cincuneta

6.

Son las seis y veinte

46

5

Where Are You Going?

- Leisure Activities Vocabulary

- Leisure Activities Dialogue and Exercises

UNIT FIVE: WHERE ARE YOU GOING?

Leisure Activities Basic Dialogue and Vocabulary, pages 49-51:

Copy and hand out these pages to introduce the vocabulary words necessary for basic communication about leisure activities. Read together with the class.

Leisure Activities Exercises, pages 52-56:

Copy and hand out pages 52, 53 and 55 for three different written and partner exercises that help students practice the new vocabulary.

Dialogue Project, page 57:

Students will prepare and perform a dialogue for the class. Use this as a good assessment tool for Units One through Five. Copy and hand out this page. Allow one class period for preparation and from 2-5 minutes for each group of two students to present their dialogue to the class.

Additional Activities:

Use oral participation with this unit. Students earn participation points for either asking or answering a question in Spanish. Keep a record of each time a student speaks.

Students' listening comprehension skills will be improving by this point in the course since they have had multiple opportunities for conversation and listening practice. As such, start speaking in Spanish about your activities of the previous day or weekend (but use the present tense). Students participate by restating, either in English or Spanish, what you said. **An example follows:**

"Yo tengo un fin de semana muy ocupado. El viernes, yo voy a una fiesta con mi familia. La fiesta es a las siete de la noche. La fiesta es por el cumpleaños de mi amiga Sofía. Sofía tiene veinticinco años. Hay muchas personas en la fiesta."

"El sábado, a las ocho y media de la mañana, yo voy al partido de fútbol de mi prima, Teresa. El partido es muy interesante. A la una de la tarde, voy al centro comercial para comprarle un regalo de cumpleaños a mi mamá. Ella tiene cincuenta y tres años."

"A las ocho de la noche, voy al cine con mi amigo José. A las diez y media de la noche, voy con José a un restaurante mexicano para comer tacos."

"El domingo, a las nueve de la mañana, voy a la iglesia. A las dos de la tarde, voy al partido de béisbol de mi hermano."

After you finish speaking, students summarize what you said. For example, "*Vas a una fiesta el viernes*", or "You go to a party on Friday." The oral participation continues until all the activities, times, days, etc., have been mentioned. Students take on the role of the narrator when they become more comfortable.

Where Are You Going?
¿Adónde vas?

Now that you know how to say the days of the week, dates, and how to tell time in Spanish, you can find out where and at what time a friend is going out. Read the following dialogue, practice it a couple of times with your partner, then switch roles.

María:	Hola, Mario.
Mario:	Hola, María. ¿Adónde vas el sábado?
María:	Voy a la fiesta con Jesús.
Mario:	¿A qué hora es la fiesta?
María:	La fiesta es a las ocho de la noche. ¿Vas conmigo?
Mario:	Sí, claro, voy a la fiesta contigo. ¡Gracias!
María:	Hasta el sábado, Mario.
Mario:	Adiós, María.

Now try to translate the dialogue into English. New vocabulary you might need is listed below:

voy a: I'm going to   *vas a:* You're going to

conmigo: with me   *contigo:* with you

la fiesta: the party   *de la noche:* at night

¡claro!: of course!   *adónde:* (to) where

con: with

Name: _____

Date: _____

Class: _____

Here are the Spanish words for some sports games you can go to:

*el partido
de básquetbol*

*el partido
de fútbol americano*

*el partido
de béisbol*

*el partido
de fútbol*

*el partido
de vólibol*

NOTE:

"*El partido*" means "the game." When referring to a particular type of game
in Spanish, you must first use "*el partido*" then "*de*" which as you already know
means "of" and finally the sport that is being played.

INCORRECT WAY: "el *béisbol partido*"

CORRECT WAY: "*el partido de béisbol*"

Where Are You Going?

Name: _____

Date: _____

Class: _____

And here are even more places that people often go to:

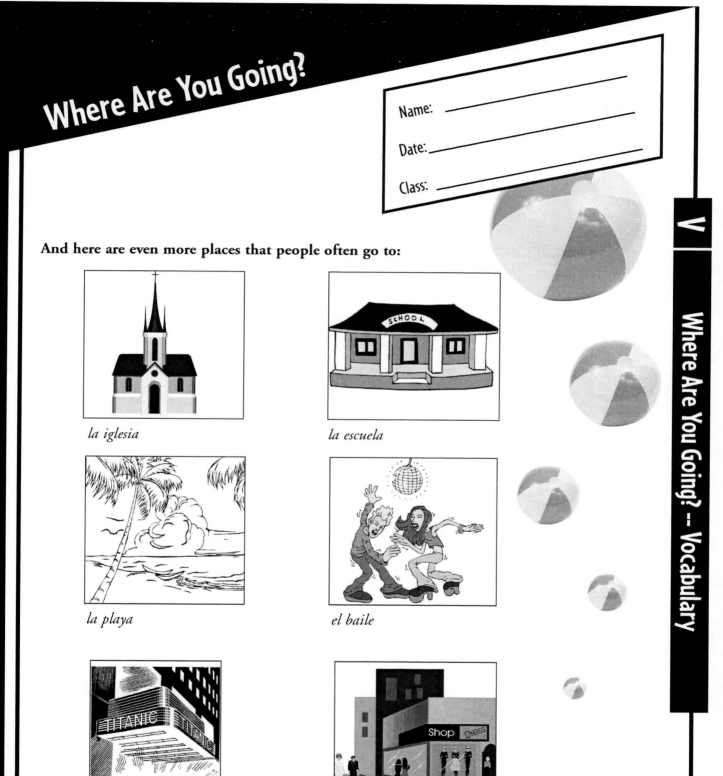

la iglesia

la escuela

la playa

el baile

el cine

el centro comercial

Name: _____

Date: _____

Class: _____

To say "I'm going" use "*(yo) voy*." To say "you're going" or to ask "are you going*?*" use "*(tú) vas*" or "*¿vas (tú)?*"

"*Voy*" and "*vas*" will always be followed by the word "*a*," which means "to" in English. The "*a*" is then followed by the place where you are going.

For example:	
(Yo) voy a la iglesia.	*(Tú) vas a la escuela.*
I'm going to church.	**You're going to school.**

Whenever the place someone is going to begins with the word "*el*," you must contract the "a" and the "*el*" to make the word "*al*."

For example:	
(Yo) voy al partido de fútbol.	*¿(Tú) vas al baile?*
I'm going to the soccer game.	**Are you going to the dance?**

Here's the rule: a + la = a la   BUT   a + el = al

Working with a partner, take turns asking each other if you are going to the following places, and then answer each other. Remember to use "*vas*" when talking to your partner and "*voy*" when talking about yourself. Don't forget the "*al*" rule above!

vas: al partido de béisbol   *vas:* _____   *vas:* _____
voy: al partido de béisbol   *voy:* _____   *voy:* _____

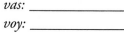

vas: a la iglesia   *vas:* _____   *vas:* _____
voy: a la iglesia   *voy:* _____   *voy:* _____

Where Are You Going?

To ask **when** people are going places, use *"¿cuándo?"*

To ask **what time** people are going places, use *"¿a qué hora?"*

For example:	*¿A qué hora vas a la escuela?*
	(At) what time are you going to school?
	¿A qué hora vas a la iglesia?
	(At) what time are you going to church?

To answer **what time** people are going places, use *"a las"* or *"a la"* + the time (*una, dos, tres y media, etc.*).

For example:	*Yo voy a la escuela a las ocho y media.*
	I am going to school at 8:30.
	Yo voy a la iglesia a las nueve y media
	I am going to church at 9:30.

In the last unit (***What Day Is It?***) you learned how to say the days of the week and the dates. Now use that vocabulary, the time vocabulary, and your new "place" vocabulary to translate the following sentences into English:

1. ¿Vas al centro comercial el sábado?

   _____

2. Voy al partido de fútbol a las dos.

   _____

3. ¿Adónde vas el fin de semana?

   _____

4. Voy a la escuela eentre semana a las ocho y treinta y cinco.

   _____

5. ¿Vas al baile el viernes conmigo?

   _____

To ask **when** people are going places, use *"¿cuándo?"*

To ask about **what time** people are going places, use *"¿a qué hora?"*

> **For example:** *¿A qué hora vas a la escuela?*
> **(At) what time are you going to school?**
>
> *¿A qué hora vas a la iglesia?*
> **(At) what time are you going to church?**

To answer **what time** people are going places, use *"a las"* or *"a la"* + the time (*una, dos, tres y media, etc.*).

> **For example:** *Yo voy a la escuela a las ocho y media.*
> **I am going to school at 8:30.**
>
> *Yo voy a la iglesia a las nueve y media*
> **I am going to church at 9:30.**

In the last unit (***What Day Is It?***) you learned how to say the days of the week and the dates. Now use that vocabulary, the time vocabulary, and your new "place" vocabulary to translate the following sentences into English:

1. ¿Vas al centro comercial el sábado?
Are you going to the mall/shopping center on Saturday?

2. Voy al partido de fútbol a las dos.
I'm going to the soccer game at 2:00.

3. ¿Adónde vas el fin de semana?
Where are you going on the weekend?

4. Voy a la escuela entre semana a las ocho y treinta y cinco.
I go to school on the weekdays (Monday through Friday) at 8:35.

5. ¿Vas al baile el viernes conmigo?
Are you going to the dance on Friday with me? / Are you going to the dance with me on Friday?

Where Are You Going?

Express the following sentences in Spanish:

Name: _____

Date: _____

Class: _____

1. I'm going to  on Thursday at 10:30.

_____

2. Are you going with me to _____ on the weekend?

_____

3. When is _____ ? I'm going with you.

_____

4. Do you go to _____ on Tuesdays?

_____

5. I'm going to _____ and on _____ Wednesday.

_____

55

Express the following sentences in Spanish:

1. I'm going to ____ on Thursday at 10:30.

Voy al centro comercial el jueves a las diez y media.

2. Are you going with me to ____ on the weekend?

¿Vas conmigo a la playa el fin de semana?

3. When is ____ ? I'm going with you.

¿Cuándo es el partido de vólibol? (Yo) voy contigo.

4. Do you go to ____ on Tuesdays?

¿Vas al partido de fútbol los martes?

5. I'm going to ____ and ____ on Wednesday.

Voy al baile y al partido de fútbol americano el miércoles.

Where Are You Going?
Dialogue Project

Name: _____

Date: _____

Class: _____

With a partner, write and perform a dialogue for the class. The dialogue will be **COMPLETELY IN SPANISH**, using the vocabulary you have reviewed and learned so far in this course. Your dialogue must contain the following:

the question, "how old are you?"
the answer to the above question
the question, "how are you?"
the answer to the above question
the question, "what time is it?"
the answer to the above question
the question, "where are you from?"
the answer to the above question
the question, "where are you going?"
the phrase "*(Yo) voy a_____*"
the phrase "*(tú) vas a_____*"
the phrase "and you?"
the phrase "with you"
the phrase "with me"
at least one expression of courtesy
at least one day of the week
at least one date, using the four-part date formula you learned
the mention of a birthday
at least one greeting word
at least one goodbye word

This project will be worth 40 points, awarded as follows:

20 points for using each of the required items
10 points for pronunciation
10 points for use of class time and readiness on the day of presentation
DIALOGUES WILL BE PERFORMED ON_____

What Do You Like to Do?

- Leisure Time Vocabulary

- Leisure Time Dialogues and Listening Activities

- Interview

- Composition

TEACHER'S Discovery

UNIT SIX: WHAT DO YOU LIKE TO DO?

Vocabulary, Exercises, and Dialogues, pages 60-63:
• Copy, hand out and review these pages. Students then complete the speaking activities on them.
• Students will need their copies of pages 50 and 51 from Unit Five to complete the dialogue.

Listening Activity, page 64:
Copy and hand out page 64 to students before you read out loud the script on page 66 to the entire class.

Interview, page 67:
Use this interview as an out-of-seat activity to see how well students are doing with their spoken responses.

Assessment, pages 68-69:
Students write their first composition as an assessment for this unit. The composition outline on page 68 and the pre-writing organizer on page 69 will help get them started.

Additional Activities:
Good activities to use with this unit are the question/answer bean bag toss and *participación oral* (described in Unit Four).

What Do You Like to Do?

¿Qué te gusta hacer?

You have just learned how to use Spanish to talk about places you go. Now you will learn some new Spanish words for activities that you may like to do:

Name: _____

Date: _____

Class: _____

jugar deportes

nadar

esquiar

montar en bicicleta

escuchar música

bailar

hablar por teléfono

viajar

hacer la tarea

60

What Do You Like to Do?

Name: _____

Date: _____

Class: _____

Here is the rest of the vocabulary you will need to talk about things you like or don't like to do:

me gusta	**I like**
te gusta	**you like**
¿te gusta?	**do you like?**
no me gusta	**I don't like**
no me gusta nada	**I really don't like**
pero	**but**

To use the phrases above, simply add the activity you are discussing at the end of the phrase.

For example:

Me gusta hablar por teléfono.
I like to talk on the phone.

No me gusta bailar.
I don't like to dance.

No me gusta nada hacer la tarea.
I really don't like to do homework.

Some other words that will be useful in conversation are:

¿Y a ti?	**And you?**	
también	**also, too**	*(used with "me gusta")*
tampoco	**either**	*(used with "no me gusta")*
¿De veras?	**Really?**	

Now, with a partner, talk about five things you like to do. Ask her if she likes to do these things, also. Take turns asking and answering the questions.

When you have finished with your first partner, find a new partner and have another conversation, this time expressing five things you don't like to do. Ask your partner if she likes to do these things, too.

What Do You Like to Do?

Name: _____

Date: _____

Class: _____

You already know how to say you are going to go somewhere (*voy a_____*) and how to ask someone if he is going to go somewhere (*¿vas a_____?*). Any of the new activities that you just learned can be used with "*voy a*" and "*vas a*" to talk about things you are going to do.

For example:

Voy a nadar el viernes.
I'm going to swim on Friday.

¿Vas a esquiar en diciembre?
Are you going to ski in December?

In the following dialogue, José and Edgar use both the new and old vocabulary you have learned to talk about what they have in common and to make plans to do something together. Practice the dialogue with a partner:

José: *Me gusta* _____ *¿Y a ti?*

Edgar: *No me gusta* _____ *pero me gusta* _____ *..*

José: *¿De veras? Me gusta* _____ *también. ¿Te gusta* _____ *? A mí me*

gusta mucho _____ *.*

Edgar: *Sí, me gusta, pero me gusta más* _____ *.*

What Do You Like to Do?

José: *¡A mí también!*   *¿Quieres ir conmigo el sábado a las dos y media?*

Edgar: *Sí, gracias, pero a las ocho voy a*   *de la clase de español.*

José: *Muy bien. ¡Hasta el sábado, Edgar!*

Edgar: *Hasta luego, José.*

Change the dialogue by substituting some of the other activities pictured on page **60**, along with different times and days of the week from the last chapter. Ask your partner if she is going to any of the places pictured on pages **50 & 51**.

After you've created a new dialogue with your partner, find a different partner and do the same thing. See how many different people you can talk with in the time you are given.

Perform your newly created dialogue for the class!

63

What Do You Like to Do?

¿Qué te gusta hacer?

Listen to your teacher read about nine people talking about their likes and dislikes. Put the number of the statement under the picture that best describes it.

Name: _____

Date: _____

Class: _____

¿Qué te gusta hacer?

Listen to your teacher read about nine people talking about their likes and dislikes. Put the number of the statement under the picture that best describes it.

3

4

5

7

6

8

2

9

1

What Do You Like to Do?
¿Qué te gusta hacer?
Script for Listening Activity

1. *Hola. Me llamo Jorge. Me gusta la escuela, y me gusta hacer la tarea.*

2. *Buenos días. Me llamo Susana. Me gusta mucho hablar por teléfono.*

3. *Hola. Me llamo Andrea. Me gusta jugar deportes.*

4. *Me llamo Jesús. No me gusta viajar, pero me gusta nadar en la playa.*

5. *Hola. Me llamo Esperanza. Me gusta esquiar en diciembre.*

6. *Hola. Me llamo Carmen. Me gusta escuchar música.*

7. *Buenos días. Soy Rogelio. Me gusta mucho montar en bicicleta los fines de semana.*

8. *Hola. Me llamo Sara. Me gusta bailar también.*

9. *Hola. Me llamo Roberto. Me gusta viajar en los Estados Unidos.*

What Do You Like to Do?

¿Qué te gusta hacer?
An interview

Ask nine of your classmates the following questions. On the line provided, record their EXACT response, then have them sign their name next to what you've written. Make sure to save your sheets for a future assignment!

Name: _____

Date: _____

Class: _____

Signature

1. ¿Te gusta escuchar música?

_____   _____

2. ¿Te gusta jugar deportes?

_____   _____

3. ¿Te gusta bailar?

_____   _____

4. ¿Te gusta hablar por teléfono?

_____   _____

5. ¿Te gusta hacer la tarea?

_____   _____

6. ¿Te gusta montar en bicicleta?

_____   _____

7. ¿Te gusta esquiar?

_____   _____

8. ¿Te gusta viajar?

_____   _____

9. ¿Te gusta nadar?

_____   _____

What Do You Like to Do?
FIRST COMPOSITION
50 POINTS

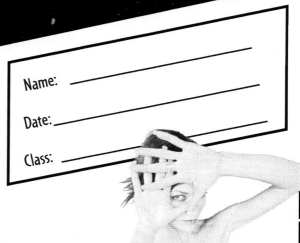

Name: _____

Date: _____

Class: _____

Use the Spanish you have learned so far to write and illustrate a short story (two paragraphs) about yourself.

In the first paragraph, tell:
1. your name
2. where you are from
3. your birth date
4. how old you are

Each correctly written complete sentence in this section is worth five points.

In the second paragraph, tell:
1. one activity you like to do a lot
2. one activity you like to do
3. one activity you don't like to do
4. one activity you really don't like to do

Each correctly written complete sentence in this section is worth five points.

Include at least one illustration pertaining to something in your story.
(an activity you like or don't like, the place you're from, etc.)

The illustration is worth 10 points if in color and five points if not in color.

The compositions will be displayed in the classroom, so be sure to do a great job!

Use the pre-writing organizer on page 69 to help you get started.

What Do You Like to Do?
First Composition Project Organizer

Name: _____

Date: _____

Class: _____

Answer the following questions in Spanish, using the questions below to help structure your composition:

1. What is your name?_____

2. How old are you?_____

3. Where are you from?_____

4. When is your birthday?_____

5. Name three activities you like to do, using *me gusta* — put them in order of preference:

_____

_____

_____

6. Name three activities that you don't like or hate to do, using *no me gusta* or *no me gusta nada*:

_____

_____

_____

7. Illustrate some things you like or don't like to do, or illustrate something else that describes you. Use color and be creative.

7

What Are You Wearing?

- **Clothing Vocabulary**

- **Adjectives & Noun/Adjective Agreement**

- **Colors**

- **Prices**

- **Quiz**

- **Oral Project/Fashion Show**

UNIT SEVEN: WHAT ARE YOU WEARING?

Clothing Vocabulary and Related Exercises, pages 72-75:

There is a variety of vocabulary and related exercises on these pages including clothing, definite article agreement, and colors. Copy, hand out and review pages 72, 73, and 74 before students complete the exercise on page 75.

Colors and Noun/Adjective Agreement, pages 77-81:

Introduce colors by first showing students colored items in the classroom and then asking them to repeat the colors in Spanish. Reinforce this unit's vocabulary by pointing out the color of students' clothing. Copy, hand out and review pages 77 and 78 before students complete the exercises on pages 79 and 81.

Prices, pages 83-84/ Adjectives, page 86/ Quiz, pages 87-92:

• Copy, hand out, and review prices on page 83, then have students complete the exercise on page 84.

• Copy, hand out and review adjectives on page 86. Then, copy and hand out pages 87-89 for a quiz on this unit.

Oral Project/Fashion Show, pages 93-95:

Copy and hand out pages 93 -94 for a description of this project, and page 95 for the rubric.

Allow at least three class days for students to prepare for the fashion show. If you don't have any "dress up" clothes in your classroom, encourage students to bring in old clothes from home to donate. Use the clothing for the skits performed in other units, since one thing middle school students LOVE to do is dress up!

Clothing Additional Activities:

Ask a student volunteer to walk around the classroom for 20 or 30 seconds, then leave the room. The other students then have one minute to record what the volunteer is wearing, using clothing vocabulary and describing it with colors. The volunteer then returns, and students see how well they did.

Another activity is for each student to anonymously write a description of his clothing, then give you the description. After all descriptions have been collected, select one description and give it to a student volunteer to read aloud. As the other students listen to the description, they look around the room to try to guess who is being described.

Numbers Additional Activity:

Play a version of "*The Price is Right*" and tape pictures of clothing to the board. Put students in pairs, with each pair receiving a list of the Spanish names of the clothing items on display, as well as their prices, written out in Spanish. The students have to match up the prices to the clothing. The pair with the most correct prices wins a prize. Encourage the students to speak only in Spanish when discussing the clothing and prices. This is a great activity for practicing multiple skills, and students are always very involved!

What Are You Wearing?

¿Qué llevas?

Here is the vocabulary you will need to discuss clothing (*la ropa*) in Spanish:

Name: _____

Date: _____

Class: _____

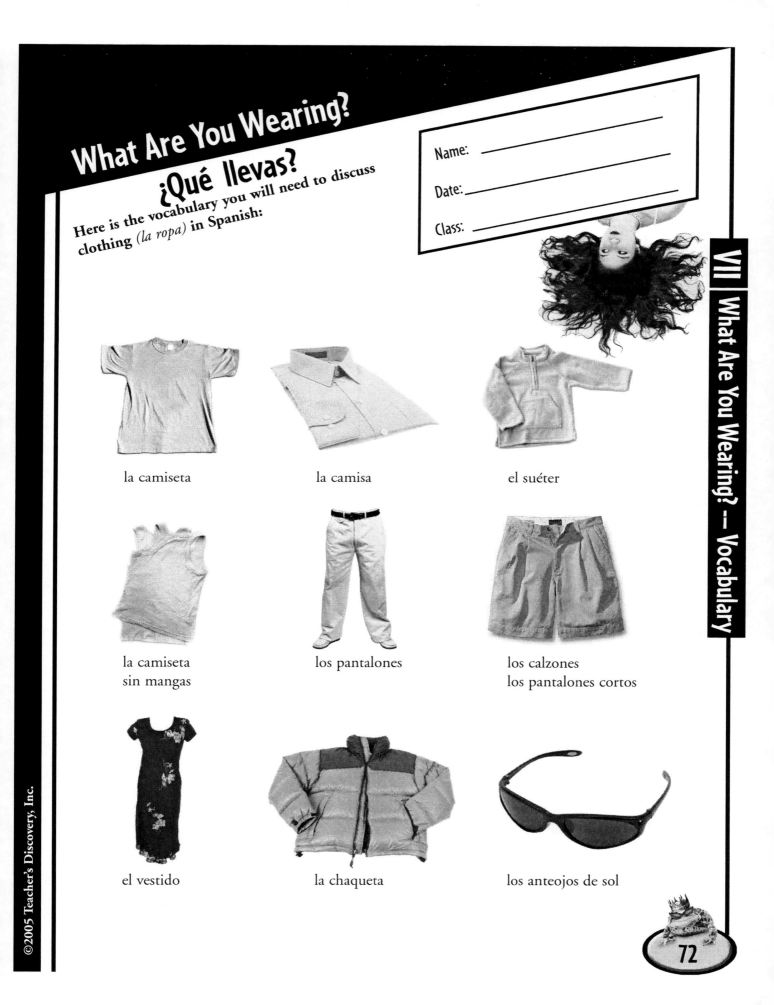

la camiseta

la camisa

el suéter

la camiseta
sin mangas

los pantalones

los calzones
los pantalones cortos

el vestido

la chaqueta

los anteojos de sol

What Are You Wearing?
¿Qué llevas?

Here is the vocabulary you will need to discuss clothing (*la ropa*) in Spanish:

Name: _____

Date: _____

Class: _____

la gorra

las sandalias

los tenis

los zapatos

las botas

los calcetines

el cinturón

el traje de baño

la bata

73

What Are You Wearing?
¿Qué llevas?

Here is the vocabulary you will need to discuss clothing (*la ropa*) in Spanish:

Name: _____

Date: _____

Class: _____

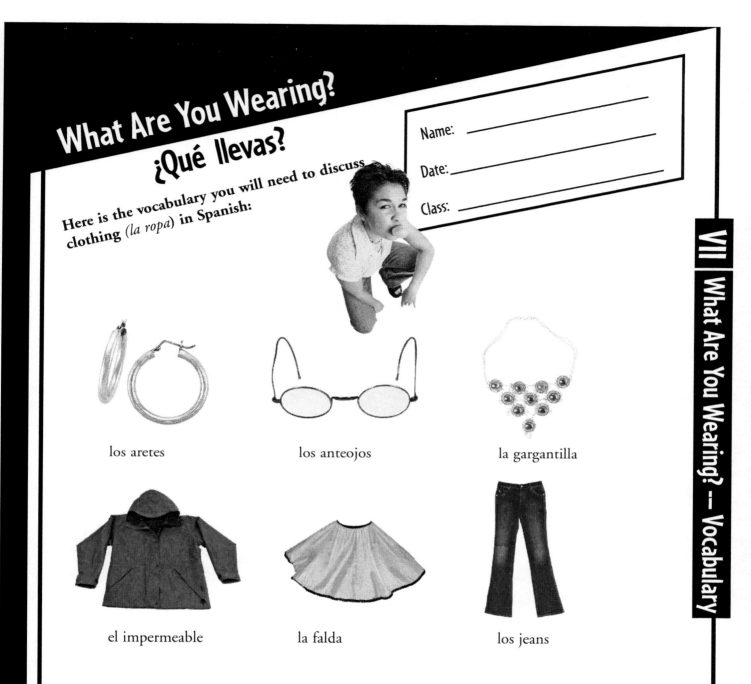

los aretes

los anteojos

la gargantilla

el impermeable

la falda

los jeans

As you can see, each article of clothing has two words: the word for "the," and the word for the type of clothing. Although English only uses one word, "the'" **Spanish uses four words for "the:" el, la, los and las.** It is very important to remember which of the four words for "the" is used with each article of clothing. Practice writing and saying each article of clothing together with its word for "the." This will help you to remember these important words.

Use the chart on page 75 to help you remember which of the four words (**el, la, los or las**) to use with the clothing vocabulary.

What Are You Wearing?
¿Qué llevas?

The four words for "the" in Spanish are called definite articles. It is very important that you remember which definite article goes with which vocabulary word. Use the chart below to categorize the articles of clothing on pages 72-74 according to their definite articles:

Name: _____

Date: _____

Class: _____

EL...
_____
_____
_____
_____

LA...
_____
_____
_____
_____
_____
_____

LOS...
_____
_____
_____
_____
_____
_____
_____
_____

LAS...
_____
_____

What Are You Wearing? - ANSWER KEY

¿Qué llevas?

The four words for "the" in Spanish are called definite articles. It is very important that you remember which definite article goes with which vocabulary word. Use the chart below to categorize the articles of clothing on page 72-74 according to their definite articles:

EL...
- vestido
- cinturón
- suéter
- traje de baño
- impermeable

LA...
- camiseta
- camiseta sin mangas
- gorra
- gargantilla
- camisa
- chaqueta
- bata
- falda

LOS...
- pantalones
- anteojos de sol
- zapatos
- aretes
- pantalones cortos
- tenis
- calcetines
- anteojos
- jeans

LAS...
- sandalias
- botas

What Are You Wearing?
Noun/Adjective Agreement

Name: _____

Date: _____

Class: _____

RULE #1: In Spanish, adjectives (words that describe) MUST always agree with the nouns (things) they are describing.

> **There are two ways that adjectives agree with nouns:**
>
> **IN NUMBER** (Singular or plural)
> **IN GENDER** (Masculine or feminine)

How do you find out what gender a word is? By the word for "the" that comes before the actual word.

For example:

MASCULINE:	FEMININE:
EL cinturón	*LA camisa*
EL traje de baño	*LA falda*

Masculine words have "*el*" before them, and feminine words have "*la*" before them. When learning new words, ALWAYS memorize the word for "the" that precedes the word, so you will always remember if a word is masculine or feminine.

To make a noun plural in Spanish, you must first make the word for "the" plural. To make *EL* plural, you change it to *LOS*. To make *LA* plural, you change it to *LAS*.

EL vestido (singular) changes to *LOS vestidos* (plural)

LA camisa (singular) changes to *LAS camisas* (plural)

When changing a word to plural, simply add an "s" to the end of the word if it ends in a vowel (A, E, I, O, U), just as you do in English.

77

What Are You Wearing?
Noun/Adjective Agreement

Name: _____

Date: _____

Class: _____

When changing a word that ends in a consonant to plural, add "es"

El suéter —— *Los suéteres*   *El cinturón* —— *Los cinturones*

How do you change the gender of an adjective (describing word)?

Adjectives that end in "o" are considered masculine, and are used to describe masculine things. If you need to describe a feminine thing, you must change the "o" at the end of the word to an "a:"

El vestido rojo   **but**   *La camisa roja*

Adjectives that end in anything other than "o" are the same for both masculine and feminine nouns:

El vestido verde   *La camisa verde*

To make adjectives plural, whether in their masculine or feminine form, just add "s" or "es," as you did with the noun!

RULE #2:   In Spanish, adjectives follow the nouns they describe. This is opposite of English, where adjectives come before the nouns they describe. For example:

The white dress ——————————— *El vestido blanco*

The yellow shoes——————————— *Los zapatos amarillos*

78

What Are You Wearing?
Noun/Adjective Agreement

Use the five colors listed below to describe the following four articles of clothing. Make sure to make the colors (adjectives) agree in number (singular or plural) and gender (masculine or feminine) with the clothing (nouns). Also, remember that the color follows the clothing. USE THE SPANISH COLORS!!!!

Name: _____

Date: _____

Class: _____

EXAMPLE: *los jeans blancos*   **(white)**

1. *el cinturón* _____ (purple)
　　el cinturón _____ (gray)
　　el cinturón _____ (green)
　　el cinturón _____ (orange)
　　el cinturón _____ (black)

2. *la falda* _____ (purple)
　　la falda _____ (gray)
　　la falda _____ (green)
　　la falda _____ (orange)
　　la falda _____ (black)

3. *los zapatos* _____ (purple)
　　los zapatos _____ (gray)
　　los zapatos _____ (green)
　　los zapatos _____ (orange)
　　los zapatos _____ (black)

4. *las botas* _____ (purple)
　　las botas _____ (gray)
　　las botas _____ (green)
　　las botas _____ (orange)
　　las botas _____ (black)

Noun/Adjective Agreement

Use the five colors listed below to describe the following four articles of clothing. Make sure to make the colors (adjectives) agree in number (singular or plural) and gender (masculine or feminine) with the clothing (nouns). Also, remember that the color follows the clothing. USE THE SPANISH COLORS!!!!

EXAMPLE: *los jeans blancos* **(white)**

1. *el cinturón* __**morado**__ (purple)
el cinturón __**gris**__ (gray)
el cinturón __**verde**__ (green)
el cinturón __**anaranjado**__ (orange)
el cinturón __**negro**__ (black)

2. *la falda* __**morada**__ (purple)
la falda __**gris**__ (gray)
la falda __**verde**__ (green)
la falda __**anaranjada**__ (orange)
la falda __**negra**__ (black)

3. *los zapatos* __**morados**__ (purple)
los zapatos __**grises**__ (gray)
los zapatos __**verdes**__ (green)
los zapatos __**anaranjados**__ (orange)
los zapatos __**negros**__ (black)

4. *las botas* __**moradas**__ (purple)
las botas __**grises**__ (gray)
las botas __**verdes**__ (green)
las botas __**anaranjadas**__ (orange)
las botas __**negras**__ (black)

What Are You Wearing?

Look at the pictures and express what you see in Spanish. Don't forget about agreement in number and gender, and to put the name of the clothing before the color.

Name: _____

Date: _____

Class: _____

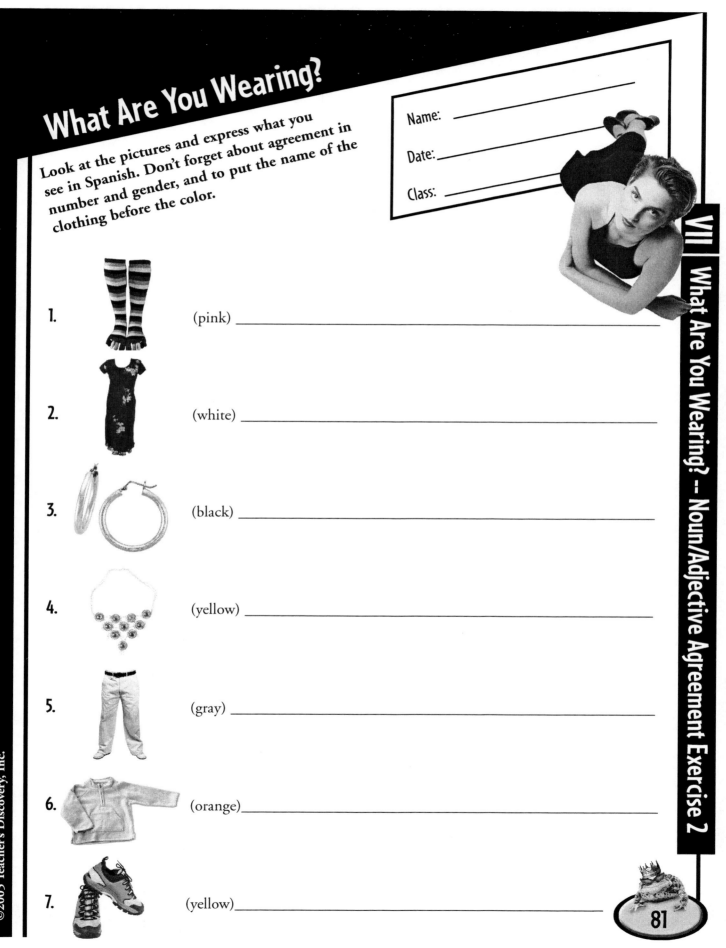

1. (pink) _____

2. (white) _____

3. (black) _____

4. (yellow) _____

5. (gray) _____

6. (orange) _____

7. (yellow) _____

Now, look at the pictures and express what you see in Spanish. Don't forget about agreement in number and gender, and to put the name of the clothing before the color.

1. (pink) _los calcetines rosados_

2. (white) _el vestido blanco_

3. (black) _los aretes negros_

4. (yellow) _la gargantilla amarilla_

5. (gray) _los pantalones grises_

6. (orange) _el suéter anaranjado_

7. (yellow) _los tenis amarillos_

What Are You Wearing?
¿Cuánto cuesta?
(How much does it cost?)

Name: _____

Date: _____

Class: _____

Now that you have learned the names of many articles of clothing and how to describe them, you will want to be able to find out how much they cost when you go to *el centro comercial*. You already know the numbers to 59. Here is the vocabulary you need to be able to count to 499:

60	70	80	90	100
sesenta...	*setenta...*	*ochenta...*	*noventa...*	*cien(to)...*
y uno	*y uno*	*y uno*	*y uno*	*uno*
y dos	*y dos*	*y dos*	*y dos*	*dos*

Just like you did with the numbers in the 20s, 30s, 40s and 50s, simply add "*y*" and a number between one and nine to add to the numbers between 60 and 99. For example, 67 would be *sesenta y siete*, and 99 would be *noventa y nueve*.

When you want to say that you have just 100 of something, use the word *cien*.

For example, *Tengo cien dólares* = **I have 100 dollars.**

However, as soon as you begin to add on to 100, you must use the word *ciento*, followed directly by the number in addition to 100, without the use of "*y*."

For example, *Tengo ciento dos dólares* = **I have 102 dollars.**

When expressing the numbers 200, 300, or 400, you simply attach the number of hundreds before the word *ciento*. For example:

200 = *doscientos*   201 = *doscientos uno*
300 = *trescientos*   335 = *trescientos treinta y cinco*
400 = *cuatrocientos*   499 = *cuatrocientos noventa y nueve*

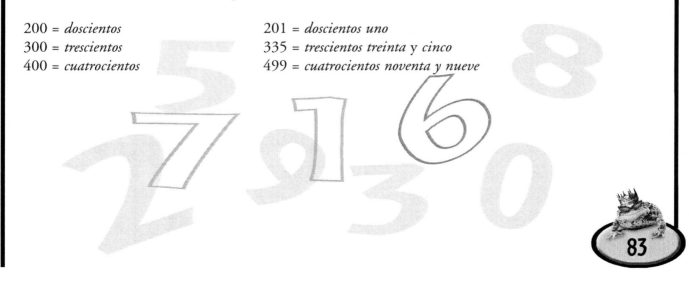

What Are You Wearing?
¿Cuánto cuesta(n)?

Use the sale items pictured below and their prices to answer the following questions in Spanish. Be sure to use the correct form of "*cuesta*" or "*cuestan*" in your complete answers.

Name: _____

Date: _____

Class: _____

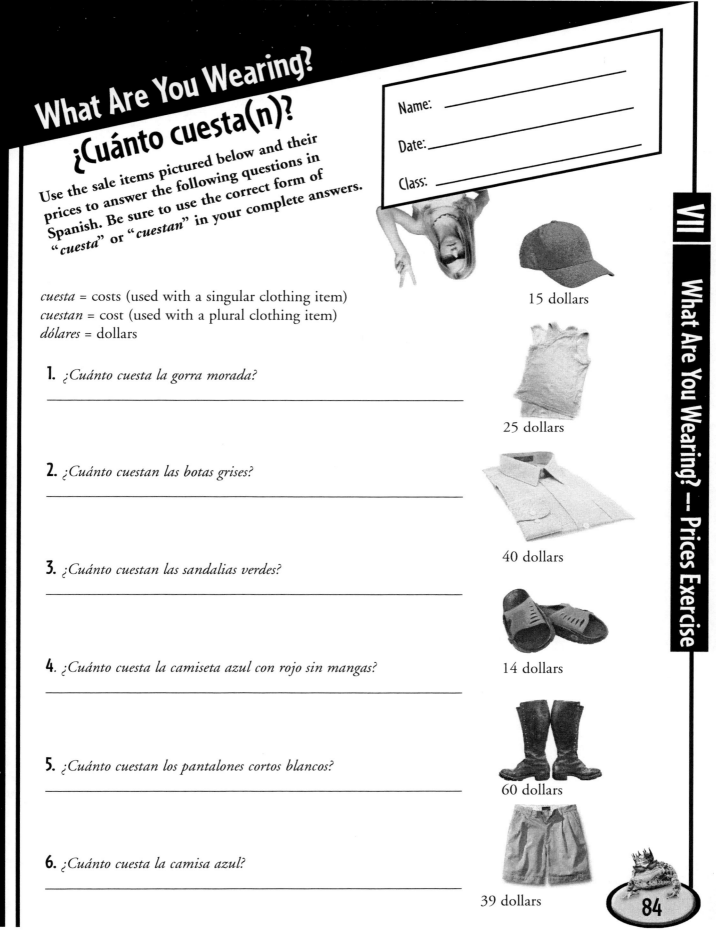

cuesta = costs (used with a singular clothing item)
cuestan = cost (used with a plural clothing item)
dólares = dollars

15 dollars

1. *¿Cuánto cuesta la gorra morada?*

_____

25 dollars

2. *¿Cuánto cuestan las botas grises?*

_____

40 dollars

3. *¿Cuánto cuestan las sandalias verdes?*

_____

4. *¿Cuánto cuesta la camiseta azul con rojo sin mangas?*

_____

14 dollars

5. *¿Cuánto cuestan los pantalones cortos blancos?*

_____

60 dollars

6. *¿Cuánto cuesta la camisa azul?*

_____

39 dollars

84

¿Cuánto cuesta(n)?

Use the sale items pictured below and their prices to answer the following questions in Spanish. Be sure to use the correct form of "*cuesta*" or "*cuestan*" in your complete answers.

cuesta = costs (used with a singular clothing item)
cuestan = cost (used with a plural clothing item)
dólares = dollars

15 dollars

25 dollars

1. *¿Cuánto cuesta la gorra morada?*

La gorra morada cuesta quince dólares.

2. *¿Cuánto cuestan las botas grises?*

Las botas grises cuestan sesenta dólares.

40 dollars

3. *¿Cuánto cuestan las sandalias verdes?*

Las sandalias verdes cuestan catorce dólares.

14 dollars

4. *¿Cuánto cuesta la camiseta azul con rojo sin mangas?*

La camiseta sin mangas azul y roja cuesta veinticinco (veinte y cinco) dólares.

5. *¿Cuánto cuestan los pantalones cortos blancos?*

Los pantalones cortos blancos cuestan treinta y nueve dólares.

60 dollars

6. *¿Cuánto cuesta la camisa azul?*

La camisa azul cuesta cuarenta dólares

39 dollars

What Are You Wearing?

Name: _____

Date: _____

Class: _____

We often use adjectives other than colors to describe clothing.
Here is a list of other adjectives that are useful in describing clothing.

Spanish Word	English Equivalent
corto	short
largo	long
caro	expensive
barato	inexpensive/cheap
pequeño	small
grande	large/big
bonito	pretty
feo	ugly
estrecho	tight
suelto	baggy

Use the word "*muy*" or "*bien*" in front of any of these adjectives to mean "very."

For example:

El vestido es muy largo.	**The dress is very long.**
Yo llevo los zapatos bien estrechos.	**I'm wearing very tight shoes.**

Remember that if an adjective ends in the letter "*o*," that means it can be changed to match the gender of the article of clothing it describes.

For example:

the short dress	**the short skirt**
el vestido corto	*la falda corta*
the short jeans	**the short boots**
los jeans cortos	*las botas cortas*

When the adjective ends in "e," it stays the same for both masculine and feminine nouns, changing only to its plural form for plural nouns.

86

What Are You Wearing?
Quiz - La ropa

Write the Spanish words for the article of clothing pictured. Don't forget to use the Spanish word for "the:" *el, la, los,* or *las.*

Name: _____

Date: _____

Class: _____

1. _____

2. _____

3. _____

4. _____

What Are You Wearing?

Quiz - La ropa

Write the Spanish words for the article of clothing pictured. Don't forget to use the Spanish word for "the:" *el, la, los,* or *las.*

Name: _____

Date: _____

Class: _____

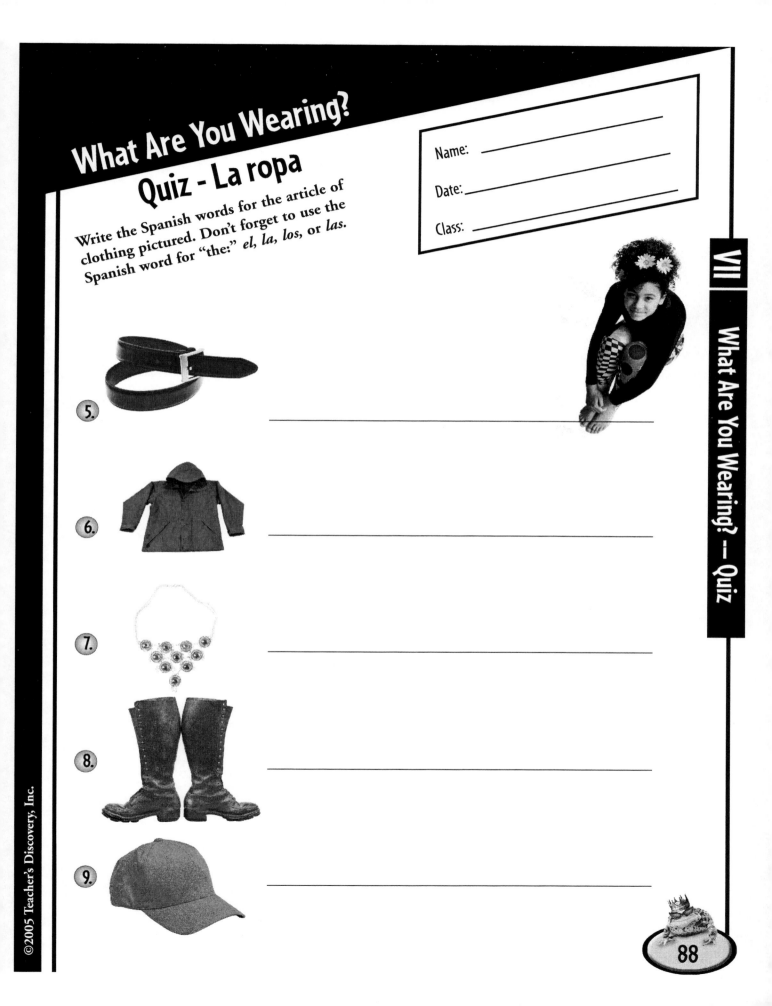

5. _____

6. _____

7. _____

8. _____

9. _____

What Are You Wearing?

Quiz - La ropa

Write the Spanish words for the article of clothing pictured. Don't forget to use the Spanish word for "the:" *el, la, los,* or *las.*

Name: _____

Date: _____

Class: _____

10. _____

11. _____

12. _____

13. _____

14. _____

Quiz - La ropa

Write the Spanish words for the article of clothing pictured. Don't forget to use the Spanish word for "the:" *el, la, los,* or *las.*

1. *la camiseta*

2. *los pantalones*

3. *los anteojos de sol*

4. *el suéter*

Quiz - La ropa

Write the Spanish words for the article of clothing pictured. Don't forget to use the Spanish word for "the:" *el, la, los,* or *las.*

5. *el cinturón*

6. *el impermeable*

7. *la gargantilla*

8. *las botas*

9. *la gorra*

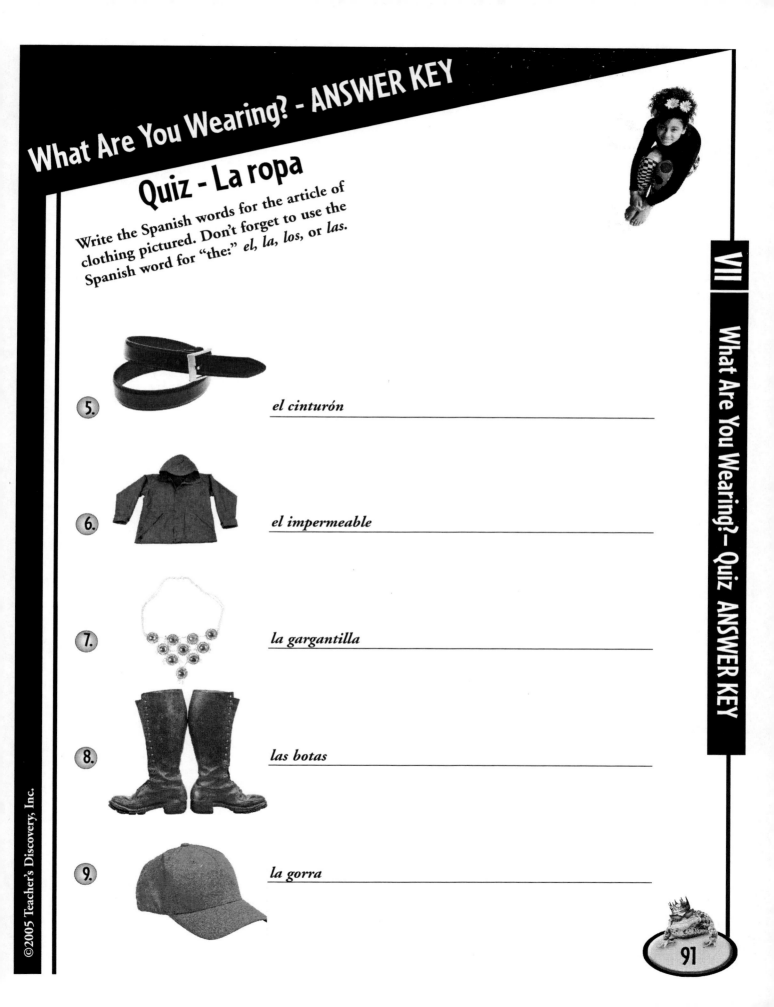

Quiz - La ropa

Write the Spanish words for the article of clothing pictured. Don't forget to use the Spanish word for "the:" *el, la, los,* or *las.*

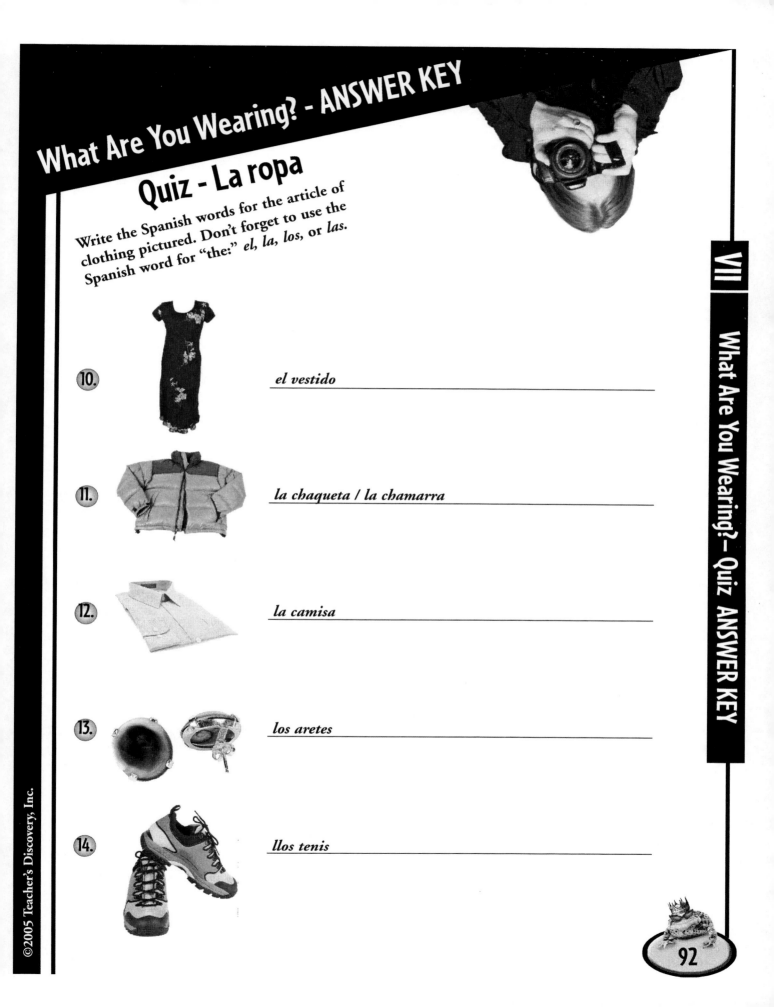

10. _el vestido_

11. _la chaqueta / la chamarra_

12. _la camisa_

13. _los aretes_

14. _llos tenis_

What Are You Wearing?
Oral Project -- La ropa

Name: _____

Date: _____

Class: _____

You will work with a partner for this project, which will be performed for the class. Select between the following three options:

OPTION I — *DESFILE DE MODAS* (FASHION SHOW) GROUPS OF TWO ONLY!

Your job is to decide on an outfit to wear for the show. This outfit must consist of at least five articles of clothing. You are responsible for writing the description of your clothing, and your partner is responsible for reading the description to the audience as you model. Each person will be graded on her own written description, and the other person will be graded on the pronunciation of the description. You will choose a name for yourself as well as a country of origin (Hispanic, of course)! Be creative — here is your chance to ham it up and have fun!

Your description must consist of:

1. At least five articles of clothing

2. The color of each article of clothing, plus additional descriptions as necessary

3. The price of the clothing in dollars. You must use the words "*cuesta*" or "*cuestan*" here.

4. Complete sentences, using the verb *lleva* (*María lleva el vestido amarillo*)

REMEMBER: if you do a fashion show, you will have to correctly pronounce the words to describe your partner's clothing. It is very unfair to your partner if your description is not ready ahead of time so your partner can practice it for the best possible pronunciation. Therefore, if your partner hasn't had ample time to practice his lines because your script was late to him, YOU will be penalized by a deduction of points. Whichever option you choose, this project involves teamwork.

What Are You Wearing?
Oral Project - La ropa

Name: _____

Date: _____

Class: _____

OPTION II - *EN EL CENTRO COMERCIAL*

With your partner, play the roles of a store clerk and a customer who wants to buy some items of clothing. Create a dialogue consisting of at least SEVEN equivalent lines of dialogue per person. Be sure to include the following:

1. Greetings

2. Asking if the store carries certain item(s) in certain colors (*¿Tienes_____?*)

3. Asking how much the item(s) costs. (*¿Cuánto cuesta(n)_____?*)

4. The use of at least two "*gusta*" expressions (*i.e., me gusta, no me gusta nada*)

5. Thank yous and goodbyes

Be creative — try having the customer buy a very ugly outfit, or the salesperson being rude, etc.

OPTION III - *EN CASA*

With two partners, pretend you are a teenager trying to convince your parents to allow you to wear a certain outfit to a party. Your parents want you to wear something else. Create a dialogue containing at least SEVEN equivalent lines of dialogue per person. Be sure to include the following:

1. At least three articles of clothing

2. Colors and other words to describe the clothing

3. Words to describe where you are going to wear the clothing (*Voy a*)

4. Words to describe why and why not the clothing should or shouldn't be worn (use of *me gusta* expressions, various adjectives, etc.)

5. Use of numbers (i.e., "but it cost _____ dollars!")

All projects REQUIRE props, clothing, and anything else you may need for your performance. Also, a written script must be typed or neatly written and turned in to your teacher BEFORE your performance. You are encouraged to use note cards.

94

What Are You Wearing?
Oral Project Scoring Rubric

Name: _____

Date: _____

Class: _____

CRITERIA	POOR (1 pt)	FAIR (5 pt)	GOOD (10 pts)
Vocabulary Use	Very limited and repetitive.	Only recently acquired vocabulary used.	Both recently acquired and previously learned vocabulary used.
Pronunciation	Poor pronunciation interferes with being understood.	Frequent mispronunciation causes some misunderstanding.	Few pronunciation errors and easily understood.
Preparation/class time use	Not ready on day of presentation — most class time spent off-task.	Somewhat unprepared on presentation day— some class time spent off-task.	Totally prepared, with script, on presentation day. All class time spent on-task.
Completion of task	Only a few of the required points included.	Most of the required points included.	All of the required points included.
Creativity	Basic presentation, with no creative additions to original assignment.Very limited and repetitive.	Expanded presentation, with one addition to original assignment.	Expanded presentation with at least two additions to original assignment.
Accuracy (x2)	Many misused words and repetitions of the same grammtical errors.	Frequent misused words and repetitions of the same grammatical errors.	Very few misused words or repetitions of the same grammatical errors.

Nombre: _____ Nota: _____

Project: _____

8

The Parts of the Body

- **Parts of the Body & Head/Face Vocabulary and Exercises**

- **Monster Drawing**

- **Adjective (Gender and Number) Agreement**

- **Written Project**

UNIT EIGHT: THE PARTS OF THE BODY

The Parts of the Body and Head/Face Vocabulary and Related Exercises, pages 98-107:

There is a variety of vocabulary and related exercises on these pages. Use these exercises to build upon vocabulary and develop larger skills, like correctly using noun/adjective agreement for both gender and number. Vocabulary sheets for this unit are on pages 98 and 101. Copy, hand out and review the vocabulary before students complete the related exercises on pages 99, 102, 104, and 106 (you will also need copies of these pages to hand out).

Monster Drawing Project, page 108:

This is a fun way to let students practice their vocabulary! They read the Spanish directions and then draw a monster based on the description provided. After they draw their monsters, collect their drawings. Later, return them to the students. Ask them to write a description of their monster as well as another student's description. For an additional activity, students work in groups of four and ask each other questions about their monsters' appearance.

Adjectives and Using Ser/Tener, pages 109-114:

Copy, hand out, and review the information on adjectives (page 109) and using *ser* and *tener* (page 110), then give students copies of the exercises to complete on pages 111 and 113.

Writing Project, pages 115-117:

Use this project to assess students' understanding of vocabulary, noun/adjective agreement, and use of "*ser*" and "*tener*." Copy, hand out, and review the materials on these pages: the project requirements and grading rubric on page 115 (and the final scoresheet on page 117) and a checklist to help guide the students on page 116.

Additional Activities:

An activity that students LOVE is the "name on the back game". Make notecards with the names of celebrities with whom students are familiar. Ask for a volunteer to come to the front of the room. While the class watches, tape a notecard to the volunteer's back, so that everyone but the student knows who the celebrity is. The volunteer's job is to guess which celebrity he is, by either asking for or listening for information from the class. Students use the new vocabulary (as well as recycled information such as age, country of origin, sports played, etc.) to describe the celebrity. After the student guesses or gives up, a new volunteer comes to the front of the room. This is a great activity that truly gets everyone involved. It is great practice for both speaking and listening.

Another great game to play in class is the board game "Guess Who?". Ask students to bring in this game from home -- many of them will have it. The object of the game is to guess who your opponent's "person" is by asking yes/no questions about that person's appearance. This is great way to review clothing vocabulary as well as use the new vocabulary from this unit.

The Parts of the Body
Las Partes Del Cuerpo

Read and practice saying these Spanish words for the parts of the body:

Name: _____

Date: _____

Class: _____

la cabeza

el cuello

el hombro

el pecho

el brazo

el codo

la mano

el estómago

la pierna

la rodilla

el pie

Remember that the definite articles "*el*" and "*la*" are used with singular nouns, and "*los*" and "*las*" are used with pluaral nouns. Many parts of the body can be referred to in either their singular or their plural forms, such as "the arm/the arms," "the foot/the feet," etc.

For a body part ending in a vowel, add an "s" to make it plural, just as you did with the clothing words. For a body part ending in a consonant, add an "es" to make it plural. Then make sure to use the appropriate definite article so that everything will agree!

The Parts of the Body

Practice changing the following body parts from singular to plural. Don't forget to change the definite article!

Example:

SINGULAR	PLURAL
el brazo	*los brazos*

1. *la rodilla* _____

2. *el pie* _____

3. *el codo* _____

4. *la mano* _____

5. *la pierna* _____

6. *el hombro* _____

7. *el brazo* _____

Now, list the body parts from the previous page that can only be singular:

1. _____

2. _____

3. _____

4. _____

The Parts of the Body - ANSWER KEY

Practice changing the following body parts from singular to plural. Don't forget to change the definite article.

Example:

SINGULAR	PLURAL
el brazo	los brazos

1. la rodilla — **las rodillas**
2. el pie — **los pies**
3. el codo — **los codos**
4. la mano — **las manos**
5. la pierna — **las piernas**
6. el hombro — **los hombros**
7. el brazo — **los brazos**

Now, list the body parts from the previous page that can only be singular:

1. **la cabeza**
2. **el estómago**
3. **el pecho**
4. **el cuello**

The Parts of the Body
Las partes de la cara
(The parts of the face)

Read and practice saying these Spanish words for the parts of the head and face:

Name: _____

Date: _____

Class: _____

el pelo

la frente

las cejas

las pestanas

los ojos

las orejas

las mejillas

la nariz

los dientes

los labios

la barbilla

The Parts of the Body

Change the following singular parts of the face and head to their plural form. Remember to change the definite articles!

Name: _____

Date: _____

Class: _____

SINGULAR	PLURAL
1. el ojo	_____
2. el diente	_____
3. el labio	_____
4. la mejilla	_____
5. la oreja	_____

Now, change the plural vocabulary back to singular:

PLURAL	SINGULAR
1. las orejas	_____
2. ojos	_____
3. las mejillas	_____
4. los dientes	_____
5. los labios	_____

102

Change the following singular parts of the face and head to their plural form. Remember to change the definite articles!

SINGULAR	PLURAL
1. el ojo	los ojos
2. el diente	los dientes
3. el labio	los labios
4. la mejilla	las mejillas
5. la oreja	las orejas

Now, change the plural vocabulary back to singular:

PLURAL	SINGULAR
1. las orejas	la oreja
2. loa ojos	el ojo
3. las mejillas	la mejilla
4. los dientes	el diente
5. los labios	el labio

The Parts of the Body

Name: _____

Date: _____

Class: _____

When referring to the parts of the face and body, Spanish almost always includes the definite article (*el, la, los,* or *las*) in addition to the body part.

Just as you did with the clothing vocabulary, simply add adjectives after the parts of the body to describe them. Also, the adjectives you use must agree in number and gender (masculine or feminine/singular or plural) with the body parts they are describing.

Use the adjectives you already know to translate the following phrases into Spanish:

1. black hair   _____

2. big eyes   _____

3. long legs   _____

4. short arms   _____

5. white teeth   _____

6. small nose   _____

7. red lips   _____

8. long hair   _____

9. large chin   _____

10. small hands   _____

When referring to the parts of the face and body, Spanish almost always includes the definite article (*el, la, los,* or *las*) in addition to the body part.

Just as you did with the clothing vocabulary, simply add adjectives after the parts of the body to describe them. Also, the adjectives you use must agree in number and gender (masculine or feminine/singular or plural) with the body parts they are describing.

Use the adjectives you already know to translate the following phrases into Spanish:

1. black hair   *el pelo negro*

2. big eyes   *los ojos grandes*

3. long legs   *las piernas largas*

4. short arms   *los brazos cortos*

5. white teeth   *los dientes blancos*

6. small nose   *la nariz pequeña*

7. red lips   *los labios rojos*

8. long hair   *el pelo largo*

9. large chin   *la barbilla grande*

10. small hands   *las manos pequeñas*

The Parts of the Body

Answer these questions in Spanish. ("*Dónde llevas?*" means "Where do you wear?")

1. *¿Dónde llevas los aretes?*
   En_____.

2. *¿Dónde llevas las sandalias?*
   En_____.

3. *¿Dónde llevas los jeans?*
   En_____.

4. *¿Dónde llevas la gorra?*
   En_____.

5. *Dónde llevas los anillos (**rings**)?*
   En_____.

6. *¿Dónde llevas las mangas?*
   En_____.

7. *¿Dónde llevas los frenos (**braces**)?*
   En_____.

8. *¿Dónde llevas los "**kneepads**?"*
   En_____.

9. *¿Dónde llevas los "**shoulderpads**?"*
   En_____.

10. *¿Dónde llevas el lápiz labial (**lipstick**)?*
    En_____.

11. *¿Dónde llevas el cinturón?*
    En_____.

12. *¿Dónde llevas "**barrettes**" y "**scrunchies**"?*
    En_____.

Answer these questions in Spanish. ("*¿Dónde llevas?*" means "Where do you wear?")

1. *¿Dónde llevas los aretes?*
En   **las orejas**   .

2. *¿Dónde llevas las sandalias?*
En   **los pies**   .

3. *¿Dónde llevas los jeans?*
En   **las piernas**   .

4. *¿Dónde llevas la gorra?*
En   **la cabeza**   .

5. *¿Dónde llevas los anillos (**rings**)?*
En   **las manos**   .

6. *¿Dónde llevas las mangas?*
En   **los brazos**   .

7. *¿Dónde llevas los frenos (**braces**)?*
En   **los dientes**   .

8. *¿Dónde llevas los "**kneepads?**"*
En   **las rodillas**   .

9. *¿Dónde llevas los "**shoulderpads?**"*
En   **los hombros**   .

10. *¿Dónde llevas el lápiz labial (**lipstick**)?*
En   **los labios**   .

11. *¿Dónde llevas el cinturón?*
En   **el estómago**   (la cintura)   .

12. *¿Dónde llevas "**barrettes**" y "**scrunchies**"?*
En   **el pelo**   .

The Parts of the Body

Read the following paragraph, then draw the monster described in the space provided below.

Name: _____

Date: _____

Class: _____

Tengo la nariz roja y tres ojos verdes y amarillos. Tengo cuatro orejas azules. Mis brazos son muy pequeños y en cada mano tengo siete dedos. Mis piernas son muy cortas y en mis pies yo llevo botas negras con calcetines anaranjados. Soy muy guapo, ¿no?

CADA = **EACH**
LLEVO = **I AM WEARING**
DEDOS = **FINGERS**

Draw here ⟶

108

The Parts of the Body
Los Adjetivos

Name:

Date:

Class:

In the last section you learned colors and other adjectives that can be used to describe clothing. Here are some additional adjectives used to describe people or body parts.

Gordo = **Fat**
Delgado = **Thin**

Fuerte = **Strong**
Débil = **Weak**

Grande = **Big/Large**
Pequeño = **Small**

Alto = **Tall**
Bajo = **Short**

Liso = **Straight**
Rizado = **Curly**

Calvo = **Bald**

Moreno = **Brunette**

Muy = **Very** (this comes before the adjective)

Feo = **Ugly**
Guapo = **Handsome/Good-looking**
Bonito = **Pretty**

Ancho = **Wide**
Estrecho = **Narrow**

Largo = **Long**
Corto = **Short**

Joven = **Young**
Viejo = **Old**

Bronceado = **Tan**

Rubio = **Blonde**

When describing a person's appearance in general, use a form of the verb "*ser*."
When describing a body part (that someone has) use a form of the verb "*tener*."
The verbs "*ser*" and "*tener*" are explained on page 110.

Remember: Adjectives come after the nouns and must agree with the nouns in number and gender.

Number = Singular or Plural
Gender = Masculine or Feminine

Name: _____

Date: _____

Class: _____

You have already used some of the forms of the verbs "*ser*" and "*tener*." Now you will learn other forms of these verbs and when to use them.

The verb "*ser*" means "to be." You have already used this verb in the phrases, "*(Yo) soy de*", and "*(Tú) eres de.*" To use these verbs to describe people, simply drop the word "*de*" from the end of the phrase:

Soy:	*(Yo) soy alto.*	I am tall.
Eres:	*(Tú) eres alto.*	You are tall.
Es:	*José es alto.*	José is tall.

The verb "*tener*" means "to have." You have also used this verb in the phrases "*(Yo) tengo trece años,*" and "*¿Cuántos años tienes (tú)?*" This verb actually means "to have." To use this verb, simply drop the word *años* from the phrase:

Tengo:	*(Yo) tengo ojos azules.*	I have blue eyes.
Tienes:	*(Tú) tienes ojos azules.*	You have blue eyes.
Tiene:	*José tiene ojos azules.*	José has blue eyes.

****IMPORTANT NOTES****

1. Use the forms of "*ser*" when describing a person in general. Use the forms of "*tener*" when describing a part of the body. In this unit, the forms of "*tener*" will always be followed by a body part.

2. Just as the clothing words had a gender (masculine or feminine), so do the words for parts of the body. **When using adjectives with body parts, the gender must agree with the gender of the body part, and NOT the gender of the person who has the body part.**

Circle the correct adjective in parentheses, making sure to match the gender (masculine or feminine) of the adjective to the gender of the noun that it describes. Then translate each sentence into English:

1. *Juan es* (gordo ó gorda)

_____.

2. *María es* (gordo ó gorda)

_____.

3. *El es* (feo ó fea)

_____.

4. *Ella es* (bonito ó bonita)

_____.

5. *José tiene el pelo* (largo ó larga)

_____.

6. *Rosa tiene el pelo* (corto ó corta)

_____.

7. *Ella es* (rubio ó rubia)

_____.

8. *El es* (moreno ó morena)

_____.

¿Cómo son estas personas?

Circle the correct adjective in parentheses, making sure to match the gender (masculine or feminine) of the adjective to the gender of the noun that it describes. Then translate each sentence into English:

1. *Juan es* ((gordo) ó gorda)

Juan is fat.

2. *María es* (gordo ó (gorda))

María is fat.

3. *Él es* ((feo) ó fea)

He is ugly.

4. *Ella es* (bonito ó (bonita))

She is pretty.

5. *José tiene el pelo* ((largo) ó larga)

José has long hair.

6. *Rosa tiene el pelo* ((corto) ó corta)

Rosa has short hair.

7. *Ella es* (rubio ó (rubia))

She is blonde.

8. *Él es* ((moreno) ó morena)

He is brunette (dark haired).

The Parts of the Body

Circle the correct adjective in parentheses by matching the gender of the nouns and adjectives and the number (singular or plural). Then, translate into English.

Name: _____

Date: _____

Class: _____

1. *Juan tiene los pies* (grande ó grandes)

_____.

2. *Ella tiene los ojos* (azul ó azules)

_____.

3. *Jorge tiene los hombros y los brazos muy* (fuerte ó fuertes)

_____.

4. *María tiene el pelo* (verde ó verdes)

_____.

5. *La chica rubia tiene la nariz* (pequeño ó pequeña)

_____.

6. *También, ella tiene las orejas* (pequeños ó pequeñas)

_____.

7. *Él tiene los dientes* (blanco ó blanca ó blancos ó blancas)

_____.

8. *La chica joven tiene los labios* (rojo ó roja ó rojos ó rojas)

_____.

Circle the correct adjective in parentheses by matching the gender of the nouns and adjectives and the number (singular or plural). Then, translate into English.

1. *Juan tiene los pies* (grande ó (grandes))

   Juan has big feet.

2. *Ella tiene los ojos* (azul ó (azules))

   She has blue eyes.

3. *Jorge tiene los hombros y los brazos muy* (fuerte ó (fuertes))

   Jorge has very strong shoulders and arms.

4. *María tiene el pelo* ((verde) ó verdes)

   María has green hair.

5. *La chica rubia tiene la nariz* (pequeño ó (pequeña))

   The blonde girl has a small nose.

6. *También, ella tiene las orejas* (pequeños ó (pequeñas))

   She also has small ears.

7. *Él tiene los dientes* (blanco ó blanca ó (blancos) ó blancas)

   He has white teeth.

8. *La chica joven tiene los labios* (rojo ó roja ó (rojos) ó rojas)

   The young girl has red lips.

The Parts of the Body
Written "EL CUERPO" Project

Name: _____

Date: _____

Class: _____

For this written project, bring in a color, full-body picture of someone. Attach the picture to unlined white paper. Use the body part vocabulary and adjectives from your workbook and write at least one paragraph describing this person in Spanish. Your description must include the following:

- **Four descriptions using the formula PERSON & FORM OF "*SER*" & ADJECTIVE**

- **Four descriptions using the formula PERSON & FORM OF "*TENER*" & BODY PART & ADJECTIVE**

* **A description of at least one article of clothing the person is wearing** (use "*yo llevo*", "*tú llevas*" or "*él/ella lleva*")

Use the PROJECT EDITING CHECKLIST (on page 116) to help you achieve the best possible project and grade.

This project is worth 60 points, based on the following rubric:

Two=SELDOM   Four=SOMETIMES   Six=USUALLY   Eight=ALWAYS

A. Followed directions
B. Used correct adjective placement
C. Used number agreement
D. Used gender agreement
E. Used "ser" correctly
F. Used "tener" correctly
G. Used correct spelling and proper punctuation

Project typed = Four points   Project not typed = Zero points

These projects will be displayed in the classroom once they are completed, so be sure to do a great job!

The Parts of the Body
"El cuerpo"
Project Editing Checklist

Name: _____

Date: _____

Class: _____

1. Did you follow the directions, and include four descriptions using "*ser*," and four descriptions using "*tener*?" Did you also describe at least one article of clothing, using "*llevar*?"

2. Did you always use a form of "*ser*" when describing just the person?

3. Did you always use a form of "*tener*" when describing the body part(s) of that person?

4. When describing a body part, did you put the adjective after the body part?

5. Do your adjectives agree in number with what you are describing? Singular body parts need a singular adjective, and plural body parts need a plural adjective:

   El ojo grande (singular)
   LoS ojoS grandeS (plural)

6. Do your adjectives agree in gender with what you are describing? Remember, when you are describing a BODY PART, the gender of the person who has that body part is unimportant.

7. Did you use correct spelling and proper punctuation?

8. Did you type your project?

116

The Parts of the Body
"El cuerpo" Project Rubric

Name: _____

Date: _____

Class: _____

NOMBRE_____

| Two=SELDOM | Four=SOMETIMES | Six=USUALLY | Eight=ALWAYS |

A. Followed directions _____/8

B. Used correct adjective placement _____/8

C. Used number agreement _____/8

D. Used gender agreement _____/8

E. Used "*ser*" correctly _____/8

F. Used "*tener*" correctly _____/8

G. Used correct spelling and proper punctuation _____/8

Project typed = Four points   Project not typed = Zero points

TOTAL: _____ **/60**

NOTA_____

The Family

- **The Family Vocabulary**

- **Possessive Adjectives**

- **Using "*Gusta*"**

- **Possessive Nouns**

- *Mi Familia* **Photo Album Project**

UNIT NINE: THE FAMILY

Vocabulary and Related Exercises, pages 120-129:

Copy, hand out, and review pages 120-123, 125, 127, and 128. Use pages 120-121 for teaching vocabulary about the family, then practice with the simple dialogue on page 122. Related exercises follow on pages 123 and 125. Page 127 introduces using possessives with nouns and a related exercise follows on page 128.

"Mi Familia" Photo Album Project, pages 130-131:

Conversing about their families during various activities in this unit will prepare students for the *"Mi Familia"* project used for assessment at the end. The project requirements are on page 130 and the accompanying rubric is on page 131.

Most students will take the family photo album project very seriously, so be sure to allow at least one full class period for students to work on the project. **Encourage students to print out digital photos or scan photos instead of bringing original photos to school, so valuable family photos are not lost.** Be sure to display the photo albums prominently in the classroom, as they provide a great opportunity to read in the target language.

Additional Activity:

Another activity that students enjoy is the family tree activity. For this activity, place the students in groups of three and tell them to choose a famous family that most other students will be familiar with (such as families from popular television sitcoms like *The Simpsons*). Tell them to draw the family tree on a sheet of paper. When they are ready, give them an overhead transparency and some markers so they can trace the drawing onto the transparency. Then, in Spanish, they must practice discussing the relationships of the family members to each other (for example, *"Homer es el padre de Bart"*). Then groups then use their transparency and the overhead to make this same presentation to the entire class. Make sure each student says at least one sentence. Encourage members of the class to ask questions, such as *¿Cómo se llama la esposa de Homer?*.

The Family
LA FAMILIA

Name: _____

Date: _____

Class: _____

Here is some Spanish vocabulary you will need to talk about the family:

mother	*la madre/la mamá*
father	*el padre/el papá*
sister	*la hermana*
brother	*el hermano*
aunt	*la tía*
uncle	*el tío*
cousin (male)	*el primo*
cousin (female)	*la prima*
stepmother	*la madrastra*
stepfather	*el padrastro*
grandmother	*la abuela*
grandfather	*el abuelo*
stepsister	*la hermanastra*
stepbrother	*el hermanastro*
son	*el hijo*
daughter	*la hija*

The Family

Name: _____

Date: _____

Class: _____

To show possession (i.e., my mother, your brother), use what are known as possessive adjectives. The four possessive adjectives you need for this unit are as follows:

SINGULAR	PLURAL
mi	mis
tu	tus

These agree in number only with the family vocabulary word to which they refer. The possessive adjectives come before the vocabulary word and replace the "*el*" or "*la*." For example:

| **my** mother | *mi madre* |
| **your** father | *tu padre* |

The plural forms are used when you are referring to more than one family member. For example:

| **my** sisters | *mis hermanas* |
| **your** brothers | *tus hermanos* |

When referring to a couple, such as parents or grandparents, use the masculine form of the vocabulary word:

my parents	*mis padres*
my grandparents	*mis abuelos*
my aunt and uncle	*mis tíos*

To talk about a mixed group of male and female family members, use the masculine plural form:

| **my** brothers and sisters | *mis hermanos* |
| **my** (boy and girl) cousins | *mis primos* |

The Family

Read the following dialogue several times with a partner, taking turns playing both roles. Then translate the dialogue into English.

Name: _____

Date: _____

Class: _____

María: Hola, Mario. ¿Qué tal?

Mario: Buenos días, María. Estoy bien. ¿Adónde vas?

María: Voy al cine con mi hermana.

Mario: ¿Cómo se llama tu hermana?

María: Ella se llama Isabel. ¿Adónde vas, Mario?

Mario: Voy al partido de fútbol de mi hermano. A mi hermano le gusta mucho jugar fútbol.

María: ¿Cómo se llama tu hermano?

Mario: Él se llama Juan. Tengo dos hermanas también.

María: Y yo también tengo dos hermanas. Mis hermanas se llaman Isabel y Ana.

Mario: Son las nueve y cuarto. El partido de fútbol es a las nueve y media. ¡Adiós, María!

María: ¡Hasta luego, Mario!

The Family

Translate the following phrases into Spanish, making sure to use the correct possessive adjective. If you are unsure which possessive adjective to use, refer to page 121.

Name: _____

Date: _____

Class: _____

1. my brother _____

2. my sisters _____

3. your aunt _____

4. your cousins (female only) _____

5. my grandmother _____

6. my grandfather _____

7. my grandparents _____

8. my brother and my parents _____

9. your sisters and your uncle _____

10. my aunt and uncle, your brothers, your sister, my stepmother and your stepfather

_____

_____

The Family - ANSWER KEY

Translate the following phrases into Spanish, making sure to use the correct possessive adjective. If you are unsure which possessive adjective to use, refer to page 121.

1. my brother __*mi hermano*__

2. my sisters __*mis hermanas*__

3. your aunt __*tu tía (su tía)*__

4. your cousins (female only) __*tus primas, (sus primas)*__

5. my grandmother __*mi abuela*__

6. my grandfather __*mi abuelo*__

7. my grandparents __*mis abuelos*__

8. my brother and my parents __*mi hermano y mis padres*__

9. your sisters and your uncle __*tus hermanas y tu tío\(sus hermanas y su tío)*__

10. my aunt and uncle, your brothers, your sister, my stepmother and your stepfather

    __*mi tía y mi tío (mis tíos), tus hermanos (sus hermanos), tu hermana*__

    __*(su hermana) mi madrastra y tu (su) padrastro*__

The Family
"GUSTA"

Name: _____

Date: _____

Class: _____

You already have learned that "*me gusta*" means "I like," and that "*te gusta*" means "you like." There are two more "*gusta*" expression you will need to talk about what someone else likes: "*le gusta*" and "*les gusta.*"

"*Le*" is used before "*gusta*" when you are referring to ONE person liking something. "*Les*" is used before "*gusta*" when you are referring to MORE THAN ONE person liking something.

When using a person's name(s) with the "*le or les gusta*" expression, you must put an "*a*" before that person's name. Read the following examples:

María likes to dance.   *A María le gusta bailar.*
María and Juan like to dance.   *A María y Juan les gusta bailar.*

Use the above examples as your guide and translate the following sentences into Spanish:

1. My brother likes to ride a bicycle.

_____

2. Susana and Gabriela like to do homework.

_____

3. My grandmother likes to ski.

_____

4. Does your grandfather like to swim?

_____

5. My cousins don't like to talk on the phone.

_____

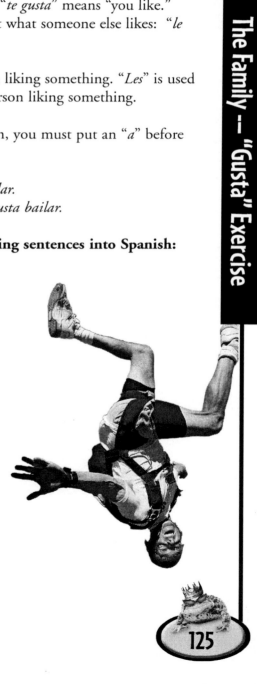

You already have learned that "*me gusta*" means "I like," and that "*te gusta*" means "you like." There are two more "*gusta*" expression you will need to talk about what someone else likes: "*le gusta*" and "*les gusta*."

"*Le*" is used before "*gusta*" when you are referring to ONE person liking something. "*Les*" is used before "*gusta*" when you are referring to MORE THAN ONE person liking something.

When using a person's name(s) with the "*le or les gusta*" expression, you must put an "*a*" before that person's name. Read the following examples:

María likes to dance. *A María le gusta bailar.*
María and Juan like to dance. *A María y Juan les gusta bailar.*

Use the above examples as your guide and translate the following sentences into Spanish:

1. My brother likes to ride a bicycle.
   A mi hermano le gusta montar en bicicleta.

2. Susana and Gabriela like to do homework.
   A Susana y a Gabriela les gusta hacer la tarea.

3. My grandmother likes to ski.
   A mi abuela le gusta esquiar.

4. Does your grandfather like to swim?
   ¿A tu abuelo (su abuelo) le gusta nadar?

5. My cousins don't like to talk on the phone.
   A mis primos no les gusta hablar por teléfono.

The Family

Name: _____

Date: _____

Class: _____

English uses an apostrophe and "s" to show possession. Spanish does not.

For example:

English:	**Mary's mother**	Correct
Spanish:	Mary's madre	Incorrect

Spanish uses a four-part formula to show possession, which is similar to the date formula you learned in Unit Three:

el, la, los or *las* + **thing possessed**   *de* + **owner of thing possessed**

Mary's dress	*el* vestido *de* Mary
Mary's skirt	*la* falda *de* Mary
Mary's shoes	*los* zapatos *de* Mary
Mary's boots	*las* botas *de* Mary

Even though people are not things and we can't actually possess them, this formula is also used when referring to people's family members:

Juan's mother	*la* madre *de* Juan
Juan's father	*el* padre *de* Juan
Juan's cousins	*los* primos *de* Juan
Juan's sisters	*las* hermanas *de* Juan

The Family

Use the four-part possession formula you just learned to translate the following phrases into Spanish. Follow the model:

Model: Pepe's mother _____*la madre de Pepe*_____

1. Susana's grandmother_____

2. José's uncle_____

3. Edmundo's parents_____

4. Juana's aunts_____

5. Rogelio's grandfather_____

6. Paco's brother_____

7. Julio's father_____

8. Cristina's stepmother_____

9. Alberto's (female) cousin_____

10. Esteban's stepsister_____

IX The Family -- Noun Possessives Exercise

Use the four-part possession formula you just learned to translate the following phrases into Spanish. Follow the model:

Model: Pepe's mother _____*la madre de Pepe*_____

1. Susana's grandmother _____*la abuela de Susana*_____

2. José's uncle _____*el tío de José*_____

3. Edmundo's parents _____*los padres de Edmundo*_____

4. Juana's aunts _____*las tías de Juana*_____

5. Rogelio's grandfather _____*el abuelo de Rogelio*_____

6. Paco's brother _____*el hermano de Paco*_____

7. Julio's father _____*el padre de Julio*_____

8. Cristina's stepmother _____*la madrastra de Cristina*_____

9. Alberto's (female) cousin _____*la prima de Alberto*_____

10. Esteban's stepsister _____*la hermanastra de Esteban*_____

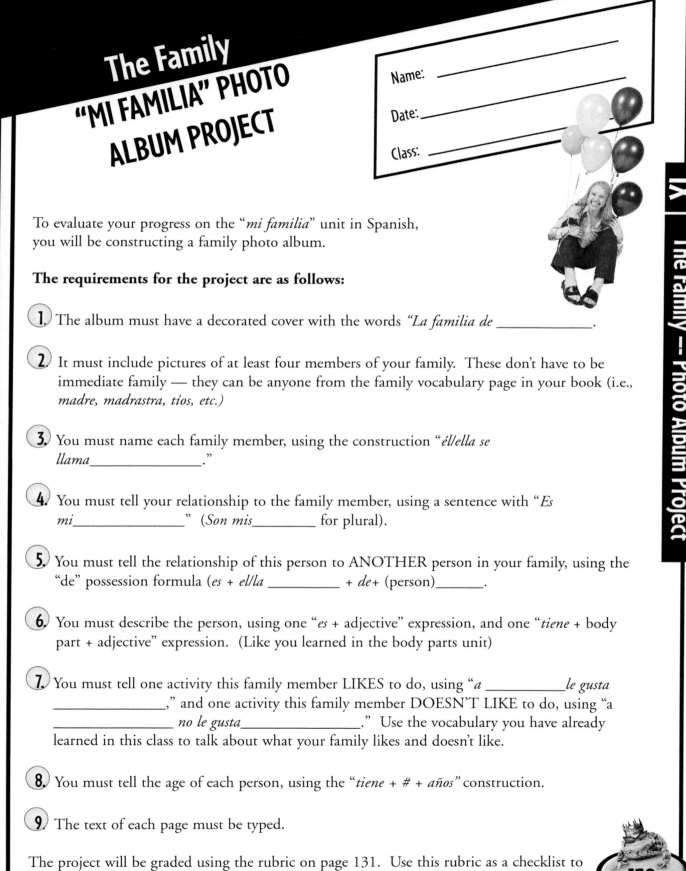

The Family
"MI FAMILIA" PHOTO ALBUM PROJECT

Name: _____

Date: _____

Class: _____

To evaluate your progress on the "*mi familia*" unit in Spanish, you will be constructing a family photo album.

The requirements for the project are as follows:

1. The album must have a decorated cover with the words "*La familia de* _____."

2. It must include pictures of at least four members of your family. These don't have to be immediate family — they can be anyone from the family vocabulary page in your book (i.e., *madre, madrastra, tíos, etc.*)

3. You must name each family member, using the construction "*él/ella se llama_____.*"

4. You must tell your relationship to the family member, using a sentence with "*Es mi_____*" (*Son mis_____* for plural).

5. You must tell the relationship of this person to ANOTHER person in your family, using the "de" possession formula (*es + el/la _____ + de*+ (person)_____.

6. You must describe the person, using one "*es + adjective*" expression, and one "*tiene + body part + adjective*" expression. (Like you learned in the body parts unit)

7. You must tell one activity this family member LIKES to do, using "*a _____le gusta _____,*" and one activity this family member DOESN'T LIKE to do, using "*a _____ no le gusta_____.*" Use the vocabulary you have already learned in this class to talk about what your family likes and doesn't like.

8. You must tell the age of each person, using the "*tiene + # + años*" construction.

9. The text of each page must be typed.

The project will be graded using the rubric on page 131. Use this rubric as a checklist to make sure you have included everything you need for the project.

The Family
"MI FAMILIA" PROJECT

Name: _____

Date: _____

Class: _____

NOMBRE: _____

Decorated, titled cover	**/10 pts**
Four family members pictured	**/10 pts**
Four "*se llama*" introductions	**/10 pts**
Four relationships using "*es mi*"	**/10 pts**
Four relationships using *el/la* ____ *de* _____	**/10 pts**
Four descriptions using "*es*" or "*tiene*"	**/10 pts**
Four "*le gusta*"	**/10 pts**
Four "*no le gusta*"	**/10 pts**
Four ages using "*tiene* _____ *años*"	**/10 pts**
Text is typed	**/10 pts**

131

10

Food and Beverages

- **Vocabulary**
- **Out-of-Seat Activity**
- **Written Activity**

UNIT TEN: FOOD AND BEVERAGES

Overview:

Since you are now at the end of the course, there are no formal assessments for this unit. This will allow time to focus on review for a comprehensive final written or oral exam.

Use plenty of *realia* in the form of play food to practice vocabulary for this unit. Give a pair of students a piece of plastic food and one minute to prepare an impromptu conversation regarding the food item.

Vocabulary plus Out-of-Seat and Written Activities, pages 134-145:

Copy, hand out and review the vocabulary and easy activities in this section to help students learn about and reinforce the names for food and beverages in Spanish.

Additional Activities:

A couple of activities that students enjoy with the food unit are writing menus and performing "restaurant" skits. Both are good assessments for this unit.

Flashcard activities are also appropriate for this unit. Put students in pairs, then give them a stack of cards with pictures or drawings of food. The cards are then spread out, face up, in front of the students. Call out the name of the food item in Spanish. Each student in the group tries to be the first to collect the matching pictured card. The student with the most cards in her pile at the end is the winner.

Another great game to help master vocabulary is "Concentration" (the memory game). For this game, place two sets of index cards on the board, face down (use magnets to hold the cards down). One side of the board contains pictured vocabulary, the other side written vocabulary. Each set of cards is a different color, and each is numbered. The students, who have been divided into two teams, take turns choosing one card from each set, comparing the pictures with the words until they get a match. Play continues until all cards have been chosen. The team with the most matched pairs is the winner.

A wonderful culminating activity is to prepare food during one of the final class periods. Have students sign up to bring in certain items and assign groups of three students to prepare different dishes. Once all the food is prepared and set up, the students enjoy their feast! Allow sufficient time for cleanup and be sure to enforce a "Spanish only" policy for the entire class period. By declaring the final class day a "Spanish only" day, students will realize and appreciate how much they have learned in your class!

Food and Beverages
La comida y las bebidas

Name: _____

Date: _____

Class: _____

In this unit, you will learn the names of the three meals in Spanish, as well as the names of many different foods and beverages. In addition to saying whether you like or don't like certain foods (you already know how to express that!) you will be able to talk about what you and others eat and drink. You will also learn some basic restaurant vocabulary, so you can order food at a Spanish-speaking restaurant.

There are three meal periods each day in Hispanic countries, just like in the United States. Meal times are roughly the same in both the United States and Hispanic countries (with the exception of dinner), although the content and size of the meals is quite different.

Name of Meal	When It's Usually Eaten:
el desayuno	*por la mañana* (7:00 - 9:00 a.m.)
el almuerzo	*por la tarde* (12:00 - 3:00 p.m.)
la comida	2:00 - 4:00 p.m.
la cena	*por la noche* (7:00 - 11:00 p.m.)

Also, most people have a snack, "*la merienda,*" at least once during the day.

Food and Beverages

Name: _____

Date: _____

Class: _____

Some words you'll need to know to talk about food and meals are:

¿Cuándo?	**when?**
¿Qué?	**what?**
para	**for**
(yo) como	**I eat**
(tú) comes	**you eat**
(yo) bebo	**I drink**
(tú) bebes	**you drink**
(yo) tengo sed	**I'm thirsty**
(yo) tengo hambre	**I'm hungry**
(tú) tienes sed	**you're thirsty**
(tú) tienes hambre	**you're hungry**
me/te gusta(n)	**I/you like**
me/te encanta(n)	**I/you love**
¡qué asco!	**how disgusting/gross**
**rico*	**tasty/delicious**
es	**(it) is**
son	**(they) are**

** *Rico* is an adjective and so it must agree in number and gender with the food or drink it describes. Write the four possible forms of *rico* below:

_____   _____

_____   _____

Now you are ready to begin learning the words for many different foods and drinks.

¡Buen Provecho!

135

Food and Beverages

Some words you'll need to know to talk about food and meals are:

¿Cuándo?	**when?**
¿Qué?	**what?**
para	**for**
(yo) como	**I eat**
(tú) comes	**you eat**
(yo) bebo	**I drink**
(tú) bebes	**you drink**
(yo) tengo sed	**I'm thirsty**
(yo) tengo hambre	**I'm hungry**
(tú) tienes sed	**you're thirsty**
(tú) tienes hambre	**you're hungry**
me/te gusta(n)	**I/you like**
me/te encanta(n)	**I/you love**
¡qué asco!	**how disgusting/gross**
**rico	**tasty/delicious**
es	**(it) is**
son	**(they) are**

** Rico is an adjective and so it must agree in number and gender with the food or drink it describes. Write the four possible forms of rico below:

rico   *rica*
_____   _____

ricos   *ricas*
_____   _____

Now you are ready to begin learning the words for many different foods and drinks.
¡Buen Provecho!

Food and Beverages
Las Frutas

Name: _____

Date: _____

Class: _____

la manzana

la naranja

la sandía

las uvas

el durazno

las cerezas

la piña

el plátano

la pera

Otras frutas que quiero probar:

137

Food and Beverages
Las verduras

Name: _____

Date: _____

Class: _____

las zanahorias

el brócoli

el elote (maíz)

el pimiento

la lechuga

las papas

el tomate

la cebolla

la coliflor

Otras verduras que quiero probar:

Name: _____

Date: _____

Class: _____

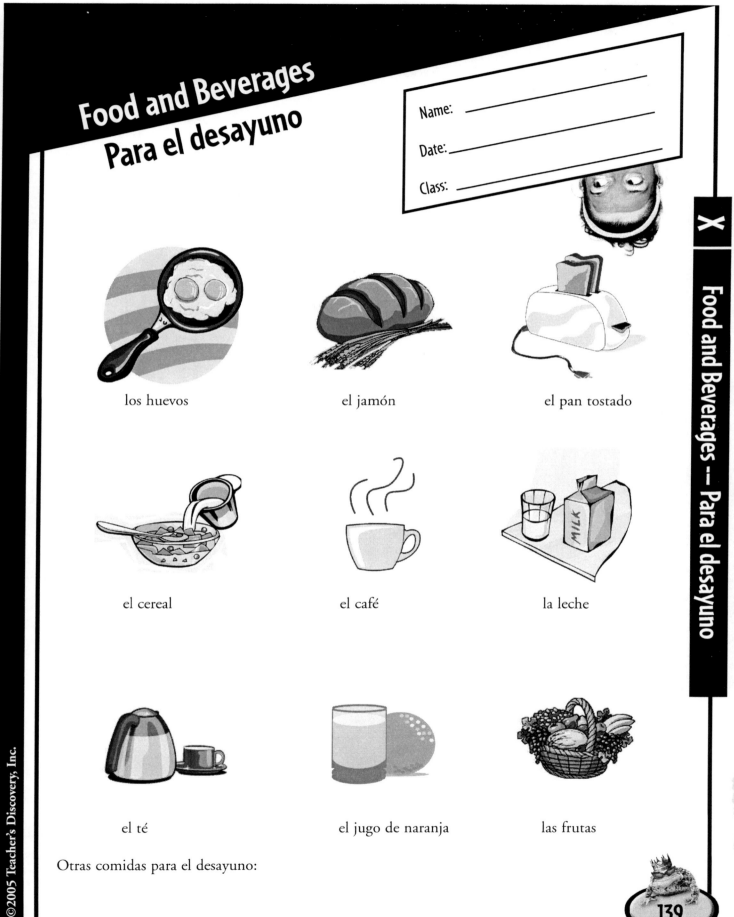

los huevos

el jamón

el pan tostado

el cereal

el café

la leche

el té

el jugo de naranja

las frutas

Otras comidas para el desayuno:

Food and Beverages
Para el almuerzo

Name: _____

Date: _____

Class: _____

la hamburguesa

el perro caliente

la pizza

el taco

el agua

el refresco

el sándwich

totopos

las papas fritas

Otras comidas para el almuerzo:

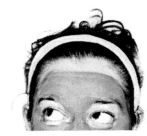

Name: _____

Date: _____

Class: _____

el pavo

el pan

el bistec

el pollo

el pescado

la ensalada

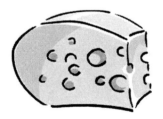

el queso

el arroz

la sopa

Otras comidas para la cena:

141

Name: _____

Date: _____

Class: _____

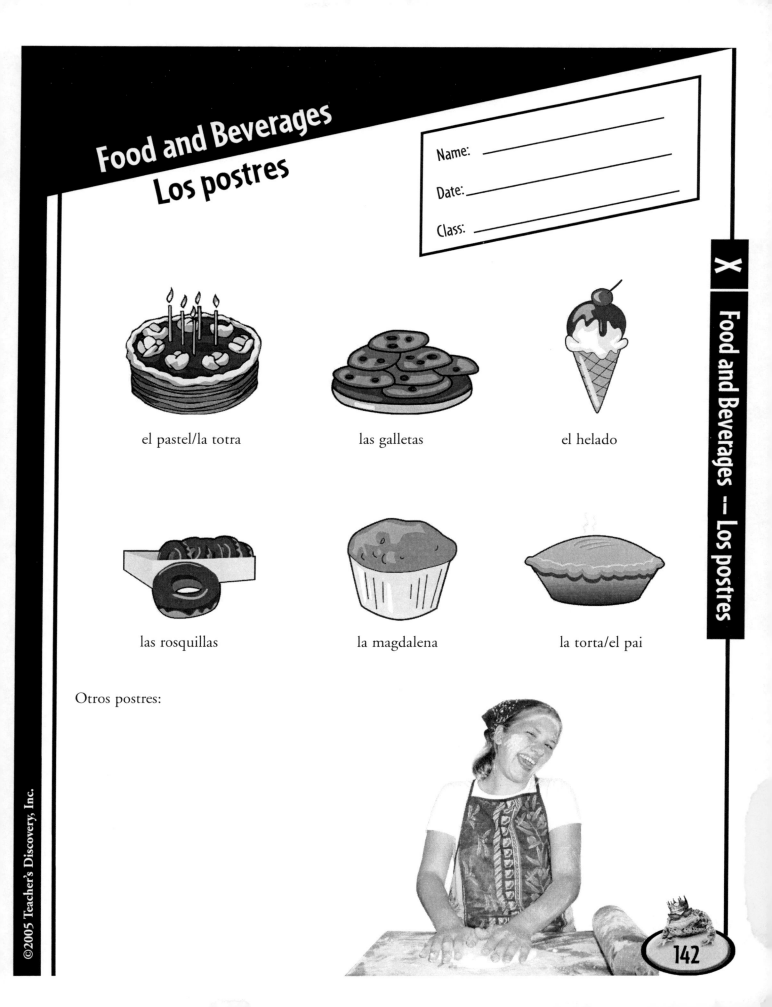

el pastel/la totra

las galletas

el helado

las rosquillas

la magdalena

la torta/el pai

Otros postres:

Food and Beverages
¿Qué te gusta comer?

Find 10 classmates who like to eat (*comer*) the following things. Ask the questions in *español*, and when you find someone to answer "*sí*," ask them to "*firma aquí, por favor.*" When you have found 10 people to sign your sheet, one for each food item, return to your seat.

Name: _____

Date: _____

Class: _____

1. ¿Te gustan las _____ ? _____

2. ¿Te gusta la _____ ? _____

3. ¿Te gusta el _____ ? _____

4. ¿Te gusta la _____ ? _____

5. ¿Te gusta el _____ ? _____

143

Food and Beverages
¿Qué te gusta comer?

Find 10 classmates who like to eat (*comer*) the following things. Ask the questions in *español*, and when you find someone to answer "*sí*," ask them to "*firma aquí, por favor.*" When you have found 10 people to sign your sheet, one for each food item, return to your seat.

Name: _____

Date: _____

Class: _____

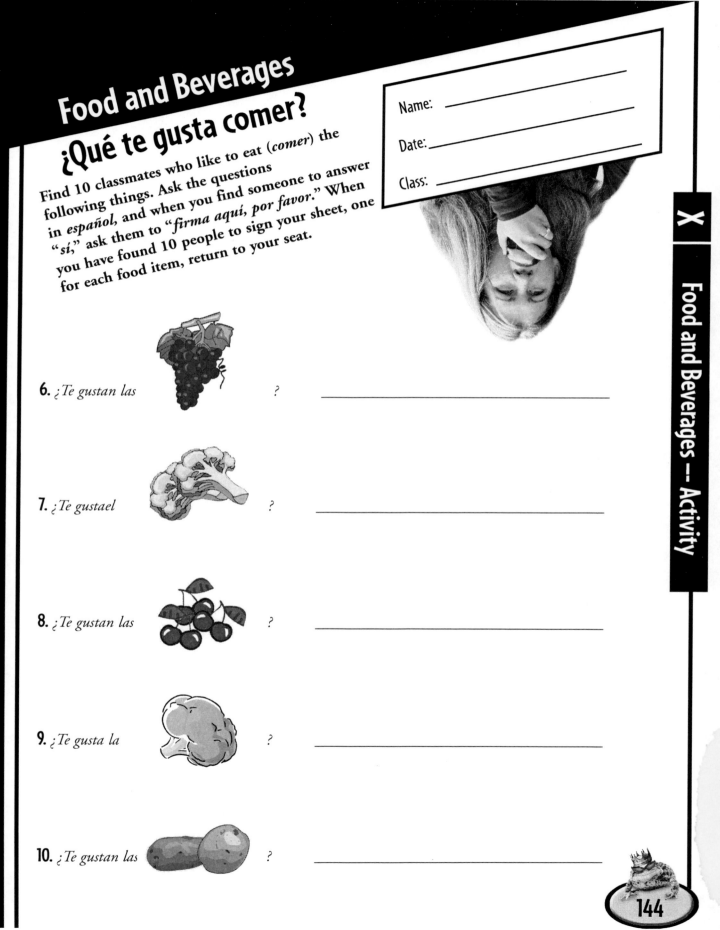

6. *¿Te gustan las* ? _____

7. *¿Te gustael* ? _____

8. *¿Te gustan las* ? _____

9. *¿Te gusta la* ? _____

10. *¿Te gustan las* ? _____